Credit Risk Management

S. K. Bagchi

JAICO PUBLISHING HOUSE

Mumbai • Delhi • Bangalore • Kolkata
Hyderabad • Chennai • Ahmedabad

Published by Jaico Publishing House
121 Mahatma Gandhi Road
Mumbai - 400 023
jaicopub@vsnl.com
www.jaicobooks.com

ISBN 81-7992-139-5

First Jaico Impression : 2004

Printed by
Uday Offset
Kewal Industrial Estate, Gala No.104, 1st Floor,
Senapati Bapat Marg, Lower Parel, Mumbai-13.

TO

MY PARENTS

WITH

PRANAM

PREFACE

Credit Risk Management is certainly not a new subject in Financial Services Industry. The 'seed' of Credit Risk with all its nuances was planted in the system long before the outgrowth of Commercial/Development Banking world over. But recent higher order emphasis and intense interest for the matter stem more out of 'commoditisation' of credit—fund-based as well as non-fund based. In the process, risk ingredients have multiplied.

BASEL Committee recognised the need of installation of the Enterprise Wide Credit Risk Management Culture and Architecture backed up with contemporary statistical tools in Banking/Financial Institutions, especially after the outbreak of Asian Financial Crisis in mid 1997. Following their advice to the Central Regulatory Authorities of the countries, RBI, in its turn, issued last year a Comprehensive Guidance Note on Management of Credit Risk to Commercial Banks for immediate adoption. For convenience of reference extracts drawn from RBI website have been placed in the Annexure.

In light of the above, there has been a general feeling that the subject of Credit Risk Management, despite retaining its fundamentals, has undergone a good deal of change for the better—more particularly, in the area of Credit Rating, Risk Models, Industry Profile studies, Credit Audit, etc. As such, the issue of revisiting the Basics of Credit Risk Management has surfaced.

PREFACE

The compendium is expected to help the Operating Personnel in Banks/Financial Institutions in their efforts of effectively implementing the directions of Regulatory Authorities. Furthermore, it is hoped that the students pursuing a course of study on Credit Risk Management may find this useful and handy.

Non-Performing Asset (NPA) Management is a separate domain though an essential component of Credit Risk Management. Hence, a Chapter has been devoted on the basics of NPA Management.

Although the book is predominantly focussed on Credit Risk, Market Risk and Operational Risk aspects have passing reference, since such Risks are linked with Credit Risk in an operating environment in some way or the other.

Glossary on Credit Risk Management has also been provided for the benefit of readers.

I shall be happy if the readers find my efforts effective in the context of the contemporary perception of the issue of Credit Risk Management.

It would also be my endeavour to present a separate book on Market Risk and Operational Risk as early as possible.

— S.K. Bagchi

ACKNOWLEDGEMENTS

I am emotionally attuned and profoundly indebted to our Great Institution—BANK OF BARODA, where I have been in, now for over three decades—for the opportunity of exposure and experience, enabling me to venture upon this humble project. I was a lucky beneficiary of a stream of encouragement from the towering personality of Late Mr. B.N. Mukherjea in the beginning, followed through Bank's stalwarts of yester years—Mr. B.K. Mukherjee, Mr. A.S. Krishnan, Mr. D.K. Mukhopadhyaya, Mr. C.B. Rammurthy, Mr. J.K. Satta—to name a few.

I am thankful to my well-wishers for the encouragement. My special thanks are due to Mr. R. Vasudevan, M.Com., CAIIB, AICWCA—a well-known Financial Analyst in the Bank—for his able assistance in case studies on Credit Rating.

I convey my sincere thanks to Mr. Akash Shah, Mr. Indranil Nandi and the entire team at Jaico Publishing House for taking keen interest and speedy action for publication of this compendium.

My daughter, Saoli—a qualified professional—has been urging upon me since long for documenting my experience in the form of a publication for use by others. This acted in me as a strong motivator.

It would be unfair on my part if I do not mention the contribution of my wife, Swati, towards the expeditious completion of the task.

TABLE OF CONTENTS

CHAPTER 1

Anatomy of Risk

1. Risk Defined
2. Risk vs Uncertainty
3. Types of Risks
4. What is Risk Management
5. Importance of Risk Management
6. Risk Philosophy vs Risk Appetite
7. Risk Management Architecture
8. Questions

INTRODUCTION

Any activity involves risk, touching all spheres of life, whether it is personal or business. For instance, if we travel by air, there is the risk of a crash; going by surface transport involves the risk of a road accident. Any business situation involves risk. To sustain its operations, a business has to earn revenue/profit and thus has to be involved in activities whose outcome may be predictable or unpredictable. There may be an adverse outcome, affecting its revenue, profit and/or capital. However, the dictum "No Risk, No Gain" holds good here. It is also aptly said that "Risks do not disappear, they give users a choice: which to retain and which to shed."

DEFINING RISK

The word RISK is derived from the Italian word *Risicare* meaning "to dare". There is no universally acceptable definition of risk. Prof. John Geiger has defined it as "an expression of the danger that the effective future outcome will deviate from the expected or planned outcome in a negative way". The Basel Committee has defined risk as "the probability of the unexpected happening—the probability of suffering a loss".

The four letters comprising the word **R I S K** define its features.

R = Rare (unexpected).

I = Incident (outcome).

S = Selection (identification).

K = Knocking (measuring, monitoring, controlling).

RISK, therefore, needs to be looked at from four fundamental aspects:

* Identification
* Measurement
* Monitoring
* Control (including risk audit)

RISK VS UNCERTAINTY

In common parlance both 'Risk' and 'Uncertainty' are used interchangeably. However, risk is to be viewed differently from mere uncertainty about the occurrence of any event in the future, since risk also involves an 'opportunity'. In other words, risk perception involves studying 'which event' is likely to happen as opposed to uncertainty, where the focus is on 'what' could take place. In a business situation, any decision could be affected by a host of events: an abnormal rise in interest rates, fall in bond prices, growing incidence of defaults by debtors, etc. A compact risk management system has to consider all these as any of them could happen at a future date, though the possibility may be low. On the other hand, if the outcome is beyond reasonable evaluation, it will be uncertainty as opposed to pure risk. Like for example the cascading effect of a technological revolution in a field not directly connected with a particular business, like the development of the electronics industry in general affecting the area of medical pathology.

TYPES OF RISKS

The risk profile of an organisation may be reviewed from the following angles:

A. Business risks:

i. Capital risk.
ii. Credit risk.
iii. Market risk.
iv. Liquidity risk.
v. Business strategy and environment risk.
vi. Operational risk.
vii. Group risk.

B. Control risks:

i. Internal controls.
ii. Organisation.
iii. Management (including corporate governance).
iv. Compliance.

Both these types of risk, however, are linked to the three omnibus risk categories listed below:

1. Credit risks.
2. Market risks.
3. Organisational risks.

Details about the types of risks are explained in subsequent chapters.

WHAT IS RISK MANAGEMENT?

The standard definition of management is that it is the process of accomplishing preset objectives; similarly, risk management aims at fulfilling the same specific objectives. This means that an organisation, whether it's a profit-seeking one or a non-profit firm, must have in place a clearly laid down parameter to contain—if not totally eliminate—the financially adverse effects of its activities. Hence, the process of identification, measurement, monitoring and control of its activities becomes paramount under risk management.

The organisation has to concentrate on the following issues:

- Creating an enabling environment across the enterprise to ensure a uniform understanding of the risk areas.
- Fixing a boundary within which the organisation will move in the matter of risk-prone activities.
- The functional authorities must limit themselves to the defined risk boundary while achieving corporate objectives.
- The risk-return equation must be such that while there is no risk aversion, the decision-making process compensates for the risk in any activity.
- The resources of the enterprise—like accounting capital (the amount put in by the owners/shareholders), regulatory capital (the amount or percentage stipulated by any regulatory authority for maintaining as a capital base) or economic capital (additional resources built up to act as a cushion for any abnormal losses)—must be consistent with the organisation's risk levels.
- There should be a balance between the organisation's risk philosophy and its risk appetite.

IMPORTANCE OF RISK MANAGEMENT

Whether it is in business or otherwise (like schools/colleges etc), risk management is not a new phenomenon. This has been there over the ages in some form or the other, though its various forms were not called market risk, credit risk or operational risk as they are today. But the importance of risk management has grown in recent times. The international regulatory authority, the Bank for International Settlements at Basel, Switzerland, has been working on a well-structured risk management system.

The concern over risk management arose from the following developments:

- In February 1995, the Barings Bank episode shook the markets and brought about the downfall of the oldest merchant bank in the UK. Inadequate regulation and the poor systems and practices of the bank were responsible for the disaster. All components of risk management—market risk, credit risk and operational risk—were thrown overboard.
- Shortly thereafter, in July 1997, there was the Asian financial crisis, brought about again by the poor risk management systems in banks/financial institutions coupled with perfunctory supervision by the regulatory authorities. Such practices could have severely damaged the monetary systems of the various countries involved and had international ramifications.

By analysing these two incidents, we can come to the following conclusions:

- Risks do increase over time in a business, especially in a globalised environment.
- A mere quantitative approach to risk perception—arising out of trading volumes, earnings levels, etc.—does not reveal the inherent drawbacks in an organisation/system.
- Increasing competition, the removal of barriers to entry to new business units by many countries, higher order expectations by stakeholders lead to assumption of risks without adequate support and safeguards.
- Businesses are tempted to bring in new types of products, spreading to uncharted areas for short-term gains.
- The traditional focus of business has been 'transaction-oriented. which has often proved disastrous. There is a need for them to take a 'risk perception' approach enterprise-wide for the long-term sustainability of operations.
- The technological revolution, while introducing countless benefits, has also created many new risks for an organisation—like technology fraud, loss due to wrong monitoring of technology etc.—which can be tackled only through a compact risk management system.
- The external operating environment in the 21st century is noticeably different. It is not possible to manage tomorrow's events with yesterday's systems and procedures and today's human skill sets. Hence risk management has to address such issues on a continuing basis and install safeguards from time to time with the tool of risk management.
- Regulatory authorities have begun to insist that organisations install a 'risk-return discipline'. This is possible only when a structured risk management environment operates in the organisation.
- Forward-looking assessment by an organisation in operational

matters is best aided by a properly articulated risk management system.

- Stakeholders in businesses are now demanding that their long-term interests be protected in a changing environment. They expect the organisation to install appropriate systems to handle a worst-case situation. Here lies the task of a risk management system—providing returns and enjoying their confidence.
- The three-pillar principle of the Basel Committee (capital adequacy, supervisory process and market discipline) can be served if an organisation has in place a risk management system.

Risk management is thus a functional necessity and adds to the strength and efficiency of an organisation on an ongoing basis.

RISK PHILOSOPHY VS RISK APPETITE

Ideally, the risk management system in any organisation must codify its risk philosophy and risk appetite in each functional area of its business. For example, in a bank or financial institution, this should specifically cover market risk, credit risk and operational risk. Risk philosophy involves developing and maintaining a healthy portfolio within the boundary set by the legal and regulatory framework. Risk appetite, on the other hand, is governed by the objective of maximising earnings within the contours of risk perception.

While coming up with a risk philosophy and a risk appetite, therefore, it is necessary to highlight the following aspects:

- They should have an enterprise-wide dimension—for example, the implications (positive or negative) of focusing on any particular business segment or other segments of the organisation.
- Calculated risk-taking should be encouraged rather than risk aversion. New and emerging business opportunities involving slightly more risks may be entertained with necessary safety belts.
- The legal and regulatory framework must be properly incorporated into the plans of the business segments with an eye, however, on maximising earnings.
- 'Adverse selection' just to prop up earnings must be avoided.

In short, risk philosophy and risk appetite must go hand-in-hand to ensure that the organisation has strength and vitality.

RISK MANAGEMENT ARCHITECTURE

The efficacy of any risk management system depends on its architecture. This comprises the following essential elements:

- A clearly defined and structured organisational set-up to manage enterprise-wide risks.
- Commitment of the highest level of those who set the policy framework and oversee implementation within the organisation—that is, the board of directors and senior management.
- Codification of risk management policies/principles, articulated in such a way that it serves the organisational risk appetite within the contours of risk perception.
- Implementing strategy of the directions through specific risk

management processes (which would include systems and procedures for operating personnel) so as to effectively identify, measure, monitor and control risk.

- Manpower development initiatives to improve the skill-sets of people in the organisation.
- Periodical evaluations.
- Risk audit.

QUESTIONS

1. *Risk and uncertainty are interchangeable and there is no difference in risk management. Do you agree? If not, state reasons.*

2. *Why are regulatory authorities advocating credit risk management in business enterprises, especially banks? Do you think an appropriate risk management architecture can reduce the impact of credit risk?*

CHAPTER 2

Risk Organisational set-up and Rationale

1. Risk Organisational Set-up
2. Principles in Risk Management
3. Risk Management Policies
4. Risk Management Process
5. Questions

RISK ORGANISATIONAL SET-UP

In a planned organisational set-up, it is necessary to keep the risk-taking and risk-control functions separate. However, while creating a balanced organisational structure, it must be borne in mind that the primary goal is not to avoid risks that are inherent in a particular business (for example, in the banking business lending is the dominant function, involving the risk of default by the borrower) but rather to steer them consciously and actively to ensure that the income generated is adequate to the assumption of risks.

In risk management, the organisational set-up must have the following elements:

- There must be clarity in the job roles of the officials.
- Inter-departmental relationships must be conducive to organisational effectiveness.
- There must be flexibility in terms of inter-connectivity of the functions of various officials: for example, the head of market risk's function is connected to that of the head of credit risk & operational risk etc.
- Control linkages and rationale.

Thus, an appropriate risk management structure is paramount in the organisation's interest. The Reserve Bank of India (RBI) has, *inter alia*, stated that "sound organisational structure is necessary for the successful implementation of risk management initiatives in an organisation" (RBI Guidance Note issued on 12 October 2002).

In limited companies, the board of directors is the highest policy-making body and has the overall responsibility for managing and controlling business risks. This role is played by the partners in partnerships, and by the board of governors in a co-operative organisation.

The board's specific roles in risk management include:

- Evolving policies based on the risk perception for the enterprise as a whole.
- Setting up risk and tolerance limits covering major risk areas for the organisation. For example, liquidity risk limit, interest rate limit, foreign exchange risk limit, credit risk limit, especially in the case of sensitive segments.
- Measuring, monitoring and controlling risk areas periodically with feedback from other operating committees.

The board is the final authority in an organisation, having the overall responsibility for growth and profitability. Therefore, to ensure compact supervision over the risk management function, a risk management committee (RMC) is usually constituted with top executives of the organisation. It may have the CEO of the company as its chairman, with directors nominated by board members.

The RMC functions as a board-level sub-committee. Its functions comprise:

- Devising operating risk policy and strategy for the entire organisation.
- Initiating measures as may be necessary from time to time

to contain risk exposures within the risk limits fixed by the board.

- Coordinating with other internal executive committees vested with managing various risk units, like the credit risk committee, asset-liability management committee (ALCO), investment committee, operational risk management committee etc. Such committees are in general responsible for implementing the directions of the RMC.

The next rungs of the risk management set-up are:

1. Credit risk management committee (CRMC), comprising heads of the credit department, investment department, treasury department and the chief economist, if there is one. The CRMC may be headed either by the CEO or by his immediate subordinate.
2. Market risk management committee/asset-liability management committee, comprising heads of treasury, foreign exchange investment, along with the chief economist if there is one. This committee may also be headed by the CEO or his immediate subordinate.
3. Operational management committee comprising heads of production (in the case of manufacturing or allied operations), various product services divisions, personnel/human resources management, internal inspection/audit & publicity or public relations etc. This committee may also be headed by the CEO or his immediate subordinate.

The functions of each of these committees (1-3) may be:

- Responsibility for the implementation of directions from the board/RMC on strategic issues.

- Monitoring relative risk sectors—for example, credit, market, operations etc.—on an enterprise-wide basis within the limits set by the board.
- Making recommendations to the board through the RMC on new thrust areas or modification of existing areas having a direct impact on the operations of the organisation in terms of earnings, capital and other areas of concern. Hence the identification, measuring, monitoring and control angles of the risk segment are to be examined and reported to the board/RMC regularly.

Since there are several types of risks involved, separate departments have to be set up to handle each one of them. These include:

- Credit risk department.
- Market risk department.
- Operational risk department.

The composition of each department depends on the size and complexity of the organisation, its risk philosophy, risk appetite and its magnitude of operations (national/international). Functionally however each department should do the following things:

- Measure, control and manage each risk area across the enterprise.
- Ensure compliance with the board's/RMC's directives on risk.
- Lay down operating instructions with a properly articulated Management Information System (MIS) and evaluation

procedure to correct deficiencies when they arise.

- Undertake portfolio studies of the external and internal environments and take steps within the framework of the organisation's operating guidelines.
- Provide support services to the RMC.

The organisational structure for risk management may vary between institutions for the following reasons:

- Differences in the size and complexity of operations.
- Varying management cultures and organisational ethos.
- Different risk philosophy and risk appetite.

Omnibus Risk Management Organisation Chart

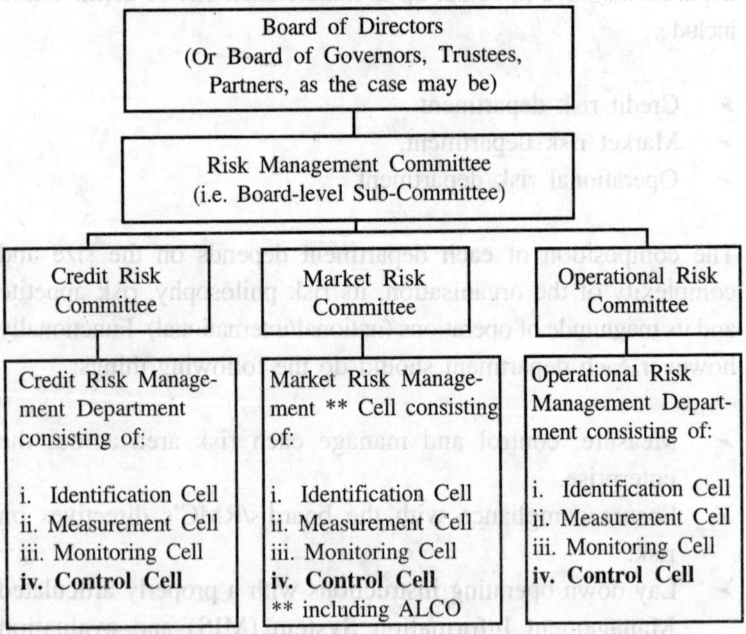

PRINCIPLES IN RISK MANAGEMENT

Any activity or group of activities needs to be done according to clear principles or 'fundamental truths'. In risk management, the following set of principles dominates an organisation's operating environment.

- Close involvement at the top level not only at the policy formulation stage but also during the entire process of implementation and regular monitoring.
- The risk element in various segments within an organisation may vary depending on the type of activities they are involved in. For example, in a bank the credit risk of loans to priority sectors may be perceived as being of 'high frequency but low value'. On the other hand, the operational risk involved in large deposit accounts may be seen as 'low frequency but high value'.
- The severity and magnitude of various types of risk in an organisation must be clearly documented. The checks and safeguards must be stated in clear terms such that they operate consistently and effectively, and allow the power of flexibility.
- There should be clear lines of responsibility and demarcation of duties of people managing the organisation.
- Staff accountability must be clearly spelt out so that various risk segments are handled by various officers with full understanding and dedication, taking responsibility for their actions.
- After identification of risk areas, it is absolutely essential that these are measured, monitored and controlled as per the needs and operating environment of the organisation. Hence, like the internal audit of financial accounts, there has to be a system of 'internal risk audit'. With regular risk

audit feedback, the principles of risk management may be laid down or changed.

- All the risk segments should operate in an integrated manner on an enterprise-wide basis.
- Risk tolerance limits for various categories must be in place and 'exception reporting' must be provided for when such limits are exceeded due to exceptional circumstances.

RISK MANAGEMENT POLICIES

Mere codification of risk principles is not enough. They need to be implemented through a defined course of action. Therefore an organisation requires policies on managing all types of risks. These have to be drawn up keeping in mind the following elements:

- The risk management process must give appropriate weightage to the nature of each risk considering the organisation's nature of business (whether purely trading, manufacturing plus trading, or financial services etc) and availability of skill sets, information systems etc. Accordingly, there should be a clear demarcation of risks and operating instructions.
- The methodology and models of risk evaluation must be built into the system.
- Action points for correcting deficiencies beyond tolerance levels must be provided for in the policy.
- Risk policy documents need not be uniform for all types of risks and, in fact, it may not be practicable. Therefore, separate policy documents have to be made for each segment—like credit risk, market risk or operational risk—within the framework of risk principles.
- An appropriate MIS is a must for the smooth and successful operation of risk management activities in an organisation.

Data collection, collation and updating must be accurate and prompt.

- The organisational structure must so designed as to fit its risk philosophy and risk appetite. Functional powers and responsibilities must be specified for the officials in charge of managing each risk segment.
- A 'back testing' process—where the quality and accuracy of the actual risk measurement is compared with the results generated by the model and corrective actions taken—must be installed.
- There should be periodical reviews—preferably on semi-annual basis—of the risk mitigating tools for each risk segment. Improvements must be initiated where necessary in the light of experience gained.
- There should be 'skilling' and 're-skilling'—and even 'de-skilling' in some cases—of various officials dealing with risk management functions in the organisation through an in-house system and/or external training programmes.
- There should be a contingent planning system to handle crisis situations that elude planned safety nets.

THE RISK MANAGEMENT PROCESS

The word 'process' connotes a continuing activity or function towards a particular result. The process is in fact the last of the four wings in the entire risk management edifice—the other three being organisational structure, principles and policies. In effect it is the vehicle to implement an organisation's risk principles and policies, aided by organisational structure, with the sole objective of creating and maintaining a healthy risk culture across the organisation.

Internationally, the risk management process has four components:

- Risk identification.
- Risk measurement.
- Risk monitoring.
- Risk control.

i. Risk identification:

In order to achieve a common understanding of the characteristics of each risk segment at all levels in an organisation, it is necessary to spell out the danger signals. This helps decision-makers to get the best from various activity points of the organisation, allowing them to take calculated risks and not be risk averse. While identifying risks, the following points have to be kept in mind.

- All types of risk (existing and potential) must be identified and their likely effect in the short-run be understood, like for example a rise in interest rates on bank borrowing in the next six months/one year.
- The magnitude of each risk segment may vary from organisation to organisation. In financial service industries like banks, delayed payments by counter-parties create 'settlement risk'. Its effects may be more severe for them when compared to utility service providers like power companies that have a wide consumer base and one default may not be a major credit risk hazard. This being so, dominant risk activities must be separated from the others in the identification process.
- The geographical area covered by an organisation may determine the coverage of its risk content. A bank that has international operations may experience different intensity of credit, market and operational risks in various countries

when compared with a pure domestic bank. Also, even within a bank, risks will vary in its domestic operations and its overseas arms.

- One clear way of identifying risk in an organisation is to scan both balance sheet items and off-balance sheet items and find the risk elements. For operational risk issues of lapses arising out of 'People', Process, System & Procedure may facilitate identification of risk contents.

ii. Risk measurement:

'Measurement' means weighing the contents and/or value, intensity, magnitude of any object against a yardstick. In risk measurement it is necessary to establish clear ways of evaluating various risk categories in an organisation, without which identification of risk would not serve any purpose. Using quantitative techniques in a qualitative framework will facilitate the following objectives.

- Finding out and understanding the exact degree of risk elements in each category in the operational environment.
- Directing the efforts of the organisation to mitigate the risks according to the vulnerability of a particular risk factor.
- Taking appropriate initiatives in planning the organisation's future thrust areas and line of business and capital allocation. The systems/techniques used to measure risk depend on the nature and complexity of a risk factor. While a very simple qualitative assessment may be sufficient in some cases, sophisticated methodological/statistical models may be necessary in others for a quantitative value. In bank lending activity, a simple one-page credit rating system along with simple financial analysis may be sufficient for a relatively low credit limit (say up to Rs 50,000). But for higher credit limits, detailed qualitative and quantitative analysis with

sophisticated credit rating models may be required because the size of the credit limit would indicate the size of default risk and its ultimate effect on the institution. Value at Risk (VAR)[1], Credit Value at Risk (C-VAR)[2], Duration[3], Stress Testing[4] are all contemporary higher-order statistical tools for the qualitative analysis of credit risk, market risk and operative risk areas.

Since an error-free risk measurement takes care of the organisation's stake and sustainability, on case-to-case basis, depending on size and complexity, statistical qualitative models may be used with the following precautions:

- The MIS in the organisation should be sufficiently compatible and reliable.
- Historical data/information should be used without any 'filtration' as otherwise proper evaluation may not be possible.
- Dominant factors of a particular risk element should be accorded a significant place and priority in the model.
- Calibration should be so undertaken that model's predicted probabilities are close to the actuals.
- "A model without sufficient validation may only be a hypothesis," wrote Roger M. Stein in *Benching Different Prediction Models*. Therefore, the results of the model should be validated from time to time.

---

1 Probability of loss on a portfolio of financial instruments over a specific time horizon, which may be even one day.

2 Value of risk in respect of a portfolio of loan over a time horizon of one year.

3 Weighted average term of cash flow from a financial instrument.

4 A process of estimating a fall in the value of a portfolio in abnormal market conditions (e.g. a market crash).

Above all, the basic inputs and assumptions in a model should be realistic after ample scrutiny and analysis.

iii. Risk monitoring:

Keeping close track of risk identification measurement activities in the light of the risk, principles and policies is a core function in a risk management system. For the success of the system, it is essential that the operating wings perform their activities within the broad contours of the organisation's risk perception. Risk monitoring activity should thus ensure that:

- Each operating segment has clear lines of authority and responsibility.
- Wherever the organisation's principles and policies are breached—even if they may be to its advantage—they should be analysed and reported to the appropriate authorities to aid in policy-making.
- In the course of risk monitoring, if it appears that it is in the organisation's interests to modify existing policies and procedures, steps to change them should be considered.
- There is an action plan to deal with major threat areas facing the organisation in the future.
- The activities of both the business and reporting wings are monitored, striking a balance at all points in time.
- Tracking of risk migrations is both upward and downward.

iv. Risk control:

There must be an appropriate mechanism to regulate or guide the operation of the risk management system in the entire organisation through a set of control devices. These can be achieved through a host of management processes such as:

- Assessing risk profile techniques regularly to examine how far they are effective in mitigating risk factors in the organisation.
- Analysing internal and external audit feedback from the risk angle and using it to activate control mechanisms.
- Segregating risk areas of major concern from other relatively insignificant areas and exercising more control over them. For example, in banks, lending against its own deposits does not pose a significant risk compared to advances against shares. In a pharmaceutical unit, quality control is riskier than credit risk.
- Putting in place a well drawn-out risk-focused audit system to provide inputs on restraint for operating personnel so that they do not take needless risks for short-term interests.
- Risk control mechanism provides top management the opportunity to review Staff Skilling (training) aspects in the organisation.

It is evident, therefore, that the risk management process through all its four wings—identification, measurement, monitoring and control—facilitates an organisation's sustainability and growth. The importance of each wing depends on the nature of organisation's activity, size and objective. But it still remains a fact that the importance of the entire process is paramount.

QUESTIONS

1. *What are the essential components of the credit risk management process?*

2. *Principles and policies in credit risk management must go hand-in-hand. Elucidate.*

3. *Draw out an organisation chart for credit risk management in a small private bank with loan/investment assets aggregating to about Rs500 crore, and average loan asset size is between Rs5 lakh and Rs10 lakh.*

CHAPTER 3

Types of Risk

1. Business Risks
2. Control Risks
3. Questions

As indicated in the first chapter, the risks that an organisation faces can be broadly divided into two categories—business risks and control risks—with further sub-divisions depending on the size, complexity and the activity of the organisation.

We shall now analyse the ingredient in each risk type so that the real impact of the risk component in each group (and sub-group) can be explained.

BUSINESS RISKS

By definition, business risks includes all risk factors, whether it affects a business directly (loss affecting capital etc.) or indirectly (continued loss affecting business strategy). Business risk can be divided into the following:

i. Capital risk:

The size of the owner's stake (like capital) in the organisation determines the strength of its operation. The composition of its capital—Tier-I (paid-up capital + reserves) and Tier-II (bonds, hybrid instruments etc.)—depends on its resource mobilisation capacity. If an organisation can access capital from only limited sources like directors (their friends and relatives) rather than from the public, then this may act as a constraint on capital. In contemporary financial management, capital has a number of components. These include:

- Accounting capital: funds belonging to the promoters/owners.
- Regulatory capital: the minimum amount of capital necessary to take care of asset value as per regulatory requirements.

- Economic capital: the amount of funds set aside to absorb any violent unexpected loss.

According to the Basel Committee, capital base is one of the three pillars of risk assessment (the other two being supervisory role and market discipline).

ii. Credit risk:

While we will discuss comprehensively on this category of risk in subsequent chapters, it may be sufficient at this stage to indicate its components:

- Credit growth in the organisation and composition of the credit folio in terms of sectors, centres and size of borrowing activities so as to assess the extent of credit concentration.
- Credit quality in terms of standard, sub-standard, doubtful and loss-making assets.
- Extent of the provisions made towards poor quality credits.
- Volume of off-balance-sheet exposures having a bearing on the credit portfolio.

iii. Market risk:

The components of this risk type are:

- Composition of the investment portfolio.
- Quality of the investment portfolio (i.e., investment in rated and unrated instruments).
- Interest rate volatility and sensibility.
- Where in a business the foreign exchange aspect is also

vital (i.e., banking/export-oriented units).

- Equity/commodity risk (i.e., hedged/unhedged components).

iv. Earnings risk:

This covers a host of items such as:

- Budget and profit planning function in the organisation.
- Analysis of income/expenses (with a focus on interest and non-interest income in case of banks/financial institutions).
- Earning quality and stability.

v. Liquidity risk:

Covers areas such as:

- Composition (wholesale/retail deposits in the case of banks with geographical and sectoral classification of depositors etc.).
- Liquidity profile (mismatch between term and non-term liabilities, behavioural maturity profile, diversification of funding sources etc.).

vi. Business strategy and environment risk:

Covers the following areas:

- External environment and macro-economic factors.
- Strategy with regard to market share, geographical spread, compatibility of strategy with in-house experience and expertise.

- Business profile analysis using SWOT (Strength, Weaknesses, Opportunities and Threats), strength of competitors, scope and diversification, extent of customer loyalty etc.
- Strategic business initiatives on the institution and streamlining of business development and proactive measures taken.
- Experience and skills of key personnel in the organisation and success in planning.
- Adequacy and compatibility of IT systems and business needs.

vii. Operational risk:

This really is an omnibus type of risk as it covers the entire gamut of activities in an organisation. The main components of operational risk are:

- People risk: the capabilities, competence and motives of the people in the organisation.
- Technology risk: system failure, system security, back-up and disaster recovery plans, IT-related frauds etc.
- Legal risk: documentation for transactions, security, compliance with customer confidentiality etc.
- Reputation risk: perception of customers and stakeholders of the organisation, regulatory perception process, strength for transaction delivery etc.
- Operating environment: abrupt non-macro economic changes in the organisation.

viii. Group risk factors:

These include

- Capital concentration of the parent/group, gearing of capital, return on capital, investment, relationship with subsidiaries, commonality of interest.
- Operating and financial performance of the subsidiaries, share of business and competition faced by subsidiaries.
- Contagious problems overlooked by the parent organisation.
- Risks arising from connected lending and intra-group exposures, risks from joint ventures, etc.
- Compliance by subsidiaries with regulatory guidelines in the area of operation.

CONTROL RISKS

In the entire risk measurement process, 'control' of activities finds a prominent place. A control mechanism is a must for any organisation's well-being. Control risks can be divided into:

i. Internal control risk:

- Lack of a clear line of responsibility and authority. In-house lack of control may lead to housekeeping and other problems, which may affect the organisation's well-being.
- Poor systems for monitoring and reporting suspicious transactions that have a noticeable impact on the organisation.
- No regular surveillance of the control mechanism by the top management.

ii. Organisational risk:

- Vague and overlapping organisational structure with unclear legal implications.
- Absence of a structured assessment mechanism to leverage external and internal relationships.
- Absence of a cordial industrial relationship.
- Lack of an adequate support system to evaluate major customer relationships.

iii. Management (including corporate governance) risk:

- Composition, cohesiveness, competence and leadership attributes of the board of directors. The match between the board and the organisation's risk philosophy and risk appetite.
- Non-assessment of the effectiveness of control functions of senior management.
- Absence of a clear succession planning mechanism.
- Undefined responsibility and accountability.
- Whether it follows contemporary corporate governance practices, especially with regard to strategy formulation and problem-solving.

iv. Risk from the compliance angle:

- Necessary emphasis not accorded to compliance with guidelines laid down by the regulatory authorities.
- Deviations not reported to the competent authorities when they arise.
- Non-adherence to a Monitorable Action Plan (MAP), if any, prescribed by a competent authority.

It is evident that all these risks are interlinked. For example, the credit risk of a bank may emerge from operational risk, where the default is the result of fraudulent activity by the bank's staff/ others or lack of care on their part. Ultimately it is reflected in the organisation's earnings (for example, losses due to credit risk, market risk and operational risk) and capital.

As omnibus categories, credit risk, market risk and operational risk cover all items of business risk and control risk. This is precisely why, internationally, risk analysis is done on these three types only.

QUESTIONS

1. *Discuss the various ingredients of business risks and control risks.*

2. *One type of risk is often linked to another. Explain with an example.*

CHAPTER 4

Nature and Scope of Credit Risk

1. "Credit"—What it includes
2. Credit Risk defined
3. Credit Risk Management—Functionality
4. Distinction between Credit Management and Credit Risk Management
5. Goal of Credit Risk Management
6. Techniques in Credit Risk Management
7. Forms of Credit Risk
8. Common causes of Credit Risk Situations
9. Conflicts in Credit Risk Management
10. Components (building blocks) of Credit Risk Management
11. Global Best Practices (Credit Risk)
12. Benefits of Best Practices
13. Questions

In the terminology of finance, the term 'credit' has an omnibus connotation. It not only includes all types of loans and advances (known as funded facilities), but also contingent items like letters of credit, guarantees and derivatives (also known as non-funded/non-credit facilities). Investment in securities is also treated as credit exposure.

WHAT IS CREDIT RISK?

'Probability of loss from a credit transaction' is the plain-vanilla definition of credit risk. In the book *Risk Management* (McGraw-Hill), Michel Crouhy *et al* have defined credit risk as "the risk of loss following a change in the factors that drive the credit quality of an asset". According to the Basel Committee, "Credit risk is most simply defined as the potential that a borrower or counter-party will fail to meet its obligations in accordance with agreed terms".

The Reserve Bank of India (RBI) has defined credit risk as "the possibility of losses associated with diminution in the credit quality of borrowers or counter-parties" (guarantors). Though credit risk is closely associated with the business of lending (that is, banks/financial institutions), it is in fact applicable to all activities where credit is involved (for example, manufacturers/traders of goods sell their products on credit to their customers). The first record of credit risk is reported to have been in 1800 B.C.

CREDIT RISK MANAGEMENT—FUNCTIONALITY

The credit risk architecture provides the broad canvas and infrastructure to effectively identify, measure, manage and control credit risk—both at the portfolio and individual levels—in accordance with an organisation's risk principles, risk policies, risk process and risk appetite as a continuous feature. It aims to strengthen and increase the efficacy of the organisation, while maintaining consistency and transparency. Beginning with the Basel Capital Accord-I in 1988 and the subsequent Barings episode in 1995 and the Asian Financial Crisis in 1997, the credit risk management function has become the centre of gravity, especially in a financial services industry like banking.

DISTINCTION BETWEEN CREDIT MANAGEMENT AND CREDIT RISK MANAGEMENT

Although credit risk management is analogous to credit management, there is a subtle distinction between the two. Here are some of the differences:

Credit Management	Credit Risk Management
1. It involves selecting and identifying the borrower/ counter-party.	1. It involves identifying and analysing risk in a credit transaction.
2. It revolves around examining the three Ps of borrowing: people (character and capacity of the borrower/ guarantor), purpose (especially if the project/purpose is viable or not), protection (security offered, borrower's capital, etc.)	2. It revolves around measuring, managing and controlling credit risk in the context of an organisation's credit philosophy and credit appetite.

Credit Management	Credit Risk Management
3. It is predominantly concerned with the probability of repayment.	3. It is predominantly concerned with probability of default.
4. Credit appraisal and analysis do not usually provide an exit feature at the time of sanction.	4. Depending on the risk manifestations of an exposure, an exit route remains an usual option through the sale of assets/securitisation.
5. The standard financial tools of assessment for credit management are balance sheet/income statement, cash flow statement, coupled with computation of specific accounting ratios. It is then followed by post-sanction supervision and a follow-up mechanism (e.g. inspection of securities, etc.).	5. Statistical tools like VaR (Value at Risk), CVaR (Credit Value at Risk), duration and simulation techniques, etc. form the core of credit risk management.
6. It is more backward-looking in its assessment, in terms of studying the antecedents/ performance of the borrower/ counterparty.	6. It is forward-looking in its assessment, looking, for instance, at a likely scenario of an adverse outcome in the business.

GOAL OF CREDIT RISK MANAGEMENT

Since the Barings Bank episode in 1995, a multitude of reasons contributed to the decline in the financial industry's credit risk situation. In this context, the Basel Committee has pointed out the following problems:

- Lax credit standards for borrowers and counterparties.
- Poor portfolio risk management.
- Lack of attention to changes in the economic situation or other circumstances that had a direct bearing on the credit standing of the counterparties.

Thus international regulatory authorities felt that a clear and well-laid risk management system is the first prerequisite in ensuring the safety and stability of the system. This involves:

- Maintaining risk-return discipline by keeping risk exposure within acceptable parameters.
- Fixing proper exposure limits keeping in view the risk philosophy and risk appetite of the organisation.
- Handling credit risk both on an 'entire portfolio' basis and on an 'individual credit or transaction' basis.
- Maintaining an appropriate balance between credit risk and other risks, like market risk, operational risk etc.
- Placing equal emphasis on 'banking book credit risk' (for example, loans and advances on the bank's balance sheet/ books), 'trading book risk' (securities/bonds) and 'off-balance sheet risk' (derivatives, guarantees, L/Cs, etc.)
- Impartial and value-added control input from credit risk management to protect capital.
- Providing a timely response to business requirements efficiently.

- Maintaining consistent quality and efficient credit process.
- Creating and maintaining a respectable and effective credit risk management culture to ensure quality credit portfolio.
- Keeping 'consistency and transparency' as the watchwords in credit risk management.

CREDIT RISK MANAGEMENT TECHNIQUES

Risk-taking is an integral part of management in an enterprise. For example, if a bank decides to lend only against its deposits, then its margins are bound to be very slender indeed. However, the bank may also not be in a position to deploy all its lendable funds, since obviously takers for loans will be very few and occasional.

The basic techniques of an ideal credit risk management culture are:

1. Certain risks are not to be taken at all even though there is the likelihood of major gains or profits, like speculative activities.
2. Transactions with a sizeable risk content should be transferred to professional risk institutions. For example, advances to small-scale industrial units and small borrowers should be covered by the Deposit & Credit Insurance Scheme in India. Similarly, export finance should be covered by the Export Credit Guarantee Scheme, etc.
3. The other risks should be managed by the institution with a proper risk management architecture.

Thus, credit management techniques are an admixture of risk avoidance, risk transfer and risk assumption. The importance of each of these will depend on the organisation's nature of activities, its size, capacity and, above all, its risk philosophy and risk appetite.

FORMS OF CREDIT RISK

Credit involves not only funds outgo by way of loans and advances and investment, but also contingent liabilities. Therefore, credit risk should cover the entire gamut of an organisation's operations whose ultimate 'loss factor' is quantifiable in terms of money.

The RBI has laid down following forms of credit risk.

1. Non-repayment of the principal of the loan and/or the interest on it.
2. Contingent liabilities like letters of credit/guarantees issued by the bank on behalf of the client and upon crystallisation—amount not deposited by the customer.
3. In the case of treasury operations, default by the counter-parties in meeting the obligations.
4. In the case of securities trading, settlement not taking place when it is due.
5. In the case of cross-border obligations, any default arising from the flow of foreign exchange and/or due to restrictions imposed on remittances out of the country.

COMMON CAUSES OF CREDIT RISK SITUATIONS

For any organisation, especially one in banking-related activities, losses from credit risk are usually very severe and not infrequent. It is, therefore, necessary to look into the causes of credit risk vulnerability. Broadly, there are **three** sets of causes:

- Credit concentration.
- Credit granting and/or monitoring process.

➢ Credit exposure in the market and liquidity-sensitive sectors.

1. Credit concentration:

Any kind of concentration has its limitations. The cardinal principle is that all eggs should not be put in the same basket. Concentrating credit on any one obligor/group or type of industry/trade can pose a threat to the lender's well-being. In the case of banking or allied functions, the extent of concentration is to be judged according to the following criteria:

- The institution's capital base (paid-up capital + reserves & surplus, etc.).
- The institution's total tangible assets.
- The institution's prevailing risk level.

The alarming consequence of concentration is the likelihood of large losses at one time or in succession without an opportunity to absorb the shock. Credit concentration may take any or both of the following forms:

i) Conventional: in a single borrower/group or in a particular sector, like steel, petroleum, etc.
ii) Common/correlated concentration: for example, exchange rate devaluation and its effect on foreign exchange derivative counter-parties.

2. Ineffective credit granting and/or monitoring process:

A strong appraisal system and pre-sanction care are the basic requisites in the credit delivery system. This again needs to be supplemented by an appropriate and prompt post-disbursement supervision and follow-up system. The history of finance is replete with cases of default due to ineffective credit granting and/or monitoring systems. Furthermore, existing systems and practices in an organisation, howsoever effective, need to be subjected to improvement from time to time in the light of developments in the marketplace.

3. Credit exposures in the market and liquidity-sensitive sectors:

Foreign exchange and derivatives contracts, letters of credit and liquidity back-up lines etc., while being remunerative, create sudden hiccups in the organisation's financial base. To guard against any rude shock, the organisation must have in place a Compact Analytical System to check for the customer's vulnerability to liquidity problems. In this context, the Basel Committee states that, "Market and liquidity-sensitive exposures, because they are probabilistic, can be correlated with credit-worthiness of the borrower. This is an important insight gained from the market turmoil in Asia, Russia in the course of 1997 and 1998."

CONFLICTS IN CREDIT RISK MANAGEMENT

An organisation dedicated to optimally manage its credit risk faces conflicts, particularly while meeting the requirements of the business sector. Its customers expect the organisation (say a bank) to extend high quality lender-service with efficiency and responsiveness, placing increasing demands in terms of higher amounts, longer tenors and lesser collateral. The organisation, on the other hand, may have a limited credit risk appetite and like to reap the maximum benefits, with lesser credit and of a shorter duration. An articulate balancing of this conflict reflects the strength and soundness of risk management practices in the organisation.

COMPONENTS (BUILDING BLOCKS) OF CREDIT RISK MANAGEMENT

The entire credit risk management edifice in an organisation (especially in a financial services industry like banking) rests upon the following three building blocks, in accordance with RBI guidelines:

i. Formulation of credit risk policy and strategy:

All organisations cannot use the same policy and strategy, even though they may be similar in many respects, whether it is nature of activity (e.g. banking), size, complexity of operations, etc. This is because each organisation has a different risk policy and risk appetite. However, one aspect that is common for any healthy organisation is that it must have an appropriate policy framework covering risk identification, measurement, monitoring and control. In such a policy initiative, there must be risk control/mitigation measures and also clear lines of authority, autonomy and accountability of operating officials. As a matter of fact, the policy document should provide flexibility to make the best use of risk-reward opportunities. Risk strategy, which is a functional element involving the implementation of risk policy, is concerned more with safe and profitable credit operations. It takes into account, *inter alia*, types of economic/business activity to which credit is to be extended, its geographical location and suitability, scope of diversification, cyclical aspects of the economy and, above all, means and ways of exiting when the risks become too high.

ii. Credit risk organisation structure:

In chapter two, we had shown an omnibus risk management organisational chart encompassing credit risk, market risk and operational risk. It also indicated that in all these three risk segments, the organisational chart should take care of the core functions of risk identification, risk measurement, risk monitoring and risk control. However, depending upon each organisation's nature of activity and, above all, its risk philosophy and risk appetite, a separate organisational chart may be constructed, combining both 'line' and 'stiff' elements.

The RBI has suggested the following pattern for banks:

- The board of directors would be in the superstructure, with a role in overall risk policy formulation and overseeing.
- There has to be a board-level sub-committee—called the Risk Management Committee (RMC)—concerned with integrated risk management. That is, framing policy issues (on the basis of the overall policy prescriptions of the board) and coming up with an implementation strategy. This sub-committee, entrusted with enterprise-wide risk management, should comprise the chief executive officer (chairman & managing director) and heads of the Credit Risk Management, and Market & Operational Risk Management Committees.
- A Credit Risk Management Committee (CRMC) should function under the supervision of the RMC. This committee should be headed by the CEO/executive director and should include heads of credit, treasury, the Credit Risk Management Department (CRMD) and the chief economist.

Functions of CRMC:

- Implementation of Credit Risk Policy.
- Monitoring credit risk on the basis of the risk limits fixed by the board and ensuring compliance on an ongoing basis.

- Seeking the board's approval for standards for entertaining credit/investment proposals and fixing benchmarks and financial covenants.
- Micro-management of credit exposures, for example risk concentration/diversification, pricing, collaterals, portfolio review, provisional/compliance aspects, etc.

Besides setting up macro-level functionaries on a committee basis, each bank is required to put in place a Credit Risk Management Department (CRMD), whose functions have been prescribed by the RBI.

Functions of CRMD:

- Measuring, controlling and managing credit risk on a bank-wide basis within the limits set by the board/CRMC.
- Enforce compliance with the risk parameters and prudential limits set by the board/CRMC.
- Lay down risk assessment systems, develop an MIS, monitor the quality of the loan/investment portfolio, identify problems, correct deficiencies and undertake loan review/audit.
- Be accountable for protecting the quality of the entire loan/investment portfolio.

iii. Credit risk operation & system framework:

Measurement and monitoring, along with control aspects, in credit risk determine the vulnerability or otherwise of an organisation while extending credit, including deployment of funds in tradable securities. As per RBI guidelines, this should involve three clear phases:

- Relationship management with the clientele with an eye on

business development.

- Transaction management involving fixing the quantum, tenor and pricing, and to document the same in conformity with statutory/regulatory guidelines.
- Portfolio management, signifying appraisal/evaluation on a portfolio basis rather than on an individual basis (which is covered by the two earlier points) with a special thrust on management of non-performing items.

In the light of all the above three phases, an organisation has to map its risk management activities (identification, measurement, monitoring and control). It has to emphasise on the following aspects:

- There should be periodical focused industry studies identifying, in particular, stagnant and dying sectors.
- Hands-on supervision of individual credit accounts through half-yearly/annual reviews of financials, position of collaterals and obligor's internal and external business environment.
- Credit sanctioning authority and credit risk approving authority to be separate.
- Level of credit sanctioning authority is to be higher in proportion to the amount of credit.
- Installation of a credit audit system in-house or handed out to a competent external organisation.
- An appropriate credit rating system to operate.
- Pricing should be linked to the risk rating of an account—higher the risk, higher the price.
- Credit appraisal and periodic reviews—together with enhancement when necessary—should be uniform, but operate flexibly.
- There should be a consistent approach (keeping in view prudential guidelines wherever existing) in the identification,

classification and recovery of non-performing accounts.

- A compact system to avoid excessive concentration of credit should operate with portfolio analysis.
- There should be a clearly laid-down process of risk reporting of data/information to the controlling/regulatory authorities.
- A conservative long provisioning policy should be in place so that all non-performing assets are provided for, not only as per the regulatory requirements, but also with some additional cushioning (some banks in India provide for a fixed percentage—usually 0.25%—of standard assets).
- There should be detailed delegation of powers, duties and responsibilities of officials dealing with credit.
- There should be a sound Management Information System.

These make it clear that operations/systems in credit risk management become really effective tools only when they are led by the principles of consistency and transparency.

GLOBAL BEST PRACTICES IN CREDIT RISK

The Basel Committee has laid down some 'best practices' in this matter:

- ➢ Establishment of an appropriate credit risk environment/culture.
- ➢ This should operate under a sound and independent credit approval process.
- ➢ Maintaining appropriate credit administration, measurement and monitoring processes.
- ➢ Ensuring adequate controls over credit risk.
- ➢ Awareness of the implications of other forms of risk, such as market risk and operational risk.
- ➢ Instilling risk-return discipline keeping in view the sophistication

of a particular type of business activity of banking.

BENEFITS OF BEST PRACTICES

The stakeholders—especially shareholders, depositors (in the case of banks) and the government—are the beneficiaries since the economic and social costs of poor credit risk practices are often huge and penetrating. Adopting globally recognised best practices strengthens confidence in the operation of the organisation concerned, besides enabling systematic peer-level analysis and comparison. It is also a fact that such practices facilitate forward-looking assessment, aided by the tools of stress testing, credit VaR etc. The end result is certainly enhanced investor confidence and returns.

QUESTIONS

1. *Define 'credit risk'. Distinguish between credit management and credit risk management.*

2. *State the common causes of credit risk concentration. Do you think conventional methods of avoiding credit risk concentration can alone ensure effective credit risk management?*

3. *The building blocks of credit risk management in an organisation reflect the quality and effectiveness of its credit risk management. Explain.*

CHAPTER 5

Accounting Ratios for Risk Evaluation

1. Overview
2. Some specific Ratios for Credit Risk Evaluation
3. Practical implications of Accounting Ratios in Credit Risk Evaluation
4. Is an Ideal Ratio an Insurance against Credit Risk?
5. Questions

AN OVERVIEW

A ratio conveys a quantitative inter-relationship between two attributes/variables for eventual comparison against a benchmark and for trend analysis. In business, accounting ratios facilitate meaningful and purpose-oriented decision-making. Its utility is determined according to the purpose for which the ratio is computed. A commercial bank may stress more on ratios like current ratio or acid test for working capital finance, while a development financial institution may consider debt-service coverage and cash flow ratios more important. An investor may, on the other hand, consider both sets of ratios equally important while a would-be employees (especially in senior positions) may evaluate a company mainly according to profit & loss ratios (net profit/sales, operating profit margin etc.) before deciding to join.

From the angle of credit risk evaluation, accounting ratios play a significant role for a lending/investing bank, since the overall computation of the credit rating of their account/exposure is aided/supported by ratio analysis also. Hence, not only is it necessary to identify relevant ratios depending on the purpose, quantum, tenure of exposure etc., but also imperative to assign weightage for the different ratios. For example, for short-term investment in marketable securities (rated by an approved external rating agency), one may focus more on current ratio/net profit/sales ratios than on long-term solvency ratios.

Internationally, there are no prescribed accounting ratios for risk evaluation. In India, too, the banking regulatory authorities have left such matters to the judgement and discretion of the banks/financial institutions concerned. However, it is logical to expect a bank/financial institution to go by established financial practices and frame an accounting ratio policy that is relevant to the purpose of its credit risk evaluation.

SOME SPECIFIC RATIOS FOR CREDIT RISK EVALUATION

For identification criteria—for example, items of current assets, current liabilities, etc.—one is to be guided by Standard Accounting Practice.

1. Short-term solvency angle:

a) Current ratio: $\frac{\text{Current assets}}{\text{Current liabilities}}$

Minimum expected level: 1.3:1

For financing working capital requirements based on the turnover method for small & medium enterprises (SMEs) and others, the minimum expected level may be 1.10:1.

b) Acid test ratio: $\frac{\text{Quick assets}}{\text{Quick liabilities}}$

Minimum expected level: 1:1

For SMEs, etc. the minimum expected level may be 0.8:1.

c) Cash ratio: $\frac{\text{Cash + bank balance + marketable securities}}{\text{Current liabilities}}$

Minimum expected level: 0.5:1

For SMEs, etc. the minimum may be lower.

2. Long-term solvency angle:

a) Debt Equity Ratio:

$$\frac{\text{Total external liabilities}}{\text{Equity (owned funds)}}$$

Maximum allowable level: 2:1

As per the Institute of Chartered Accountants of India, there can be no maximum debt:equity ratio, when 'debt' represents only long-term borrowed funds. It varies from case to case.

Higher levels may be allowed for the infrastructure sector (5:1), priority sector like SSIs/SMEs, etc. (4:1) and other sectors having specific factors, like ship-breaking units, etc.

b) Debt service coverage ratio:

$$\frac{\text{Earnings available for debt service}}{\text{One-year debt instalment payment + interest thereon}}$$

Earnings include: Net profit

Plus

- Depreciation on fixed assets
- Loss, if any, on the sale of fixed assets
- Interest on debt for one year

Minimum expected level: 1.50:1

For priority sector, SMEs, etc., as stated above, this minimum may be allowed at 1.30:1.

3. Profitability angle:

a) Operating profit ratio:

$$\frac{\text{Profit before deduction of depreciation, tax \& finance charges}}{\text{Sales/income}}$$

The expected level will depend upon the nature of the industry/ business, operational area, size of the unit, the duration of the business being carried on, trend analysis and other relevant factors. However, a good unit is likely to show at least a margin of 25-30%.

b) Return on capital employed (ROCE) ratio:

$$\frac{\text{Operating profit}}{\text{Owned funds + long-term loan funds}}$$

The expected level will be based on factors as stated in 3(a) above. However, ordinarily it is likely to be at least 15-20%.

c) Interest coverage ratio: $\frac{\text{Operating profit}}{\text{Interest liability}}$

Subject to factors as stated in 3(a) above.

d) Profit-asset ratio: $\frac{\text{Operating profit}}{\text{Total tangible assets}}$

The minimum expected level will depend upon factors as stated in 3(a) above.

e) Indirect overhead ratio:

$$\frac{\text{Finance charges + depreciation (on fixed assets used for administrative/office purposes) + Selling \& administrative cost}}{\text{Sales/income}}$$

The maximum allowable level is to be decided on a case-by-case basis based on 3(a) above. However, it may be 10-15%.

4. From the asset movement angle:

a) $\frac{\text{Inventory holding x 300 days **}}{\text{Sales}}$

b) $\frac{\text{Trade debtors x 300 days ** (preferably average outstanding in a year)}}{\text{Sales/Income}}$

5. Trade credit payment angle:

$$\frac{\text{Trade creditors x 300 days ** (preferably average outstanding in a year)}}{\text{Credit purchase of current assets (preferably average level in a year)}}$$

** Computation based on 300 days in a year is advisable in the Indian context keeping in view the usual 52 weekly offs, national holidays, etc.

The expected level varies from case to case as stated in 3(a) above. However, generally, the maximum level in terms of days may be between 90 and 120.

6. From the 'stress' angle:

(The Basel Committee states: "Stress testing has been adopted as a generic term describing various techniques used by banks to gauge their potential vulnerability to exceptional, but plausible, events.")

$$\frac{\text{Stress tested cash flow}}{\text{Debt payments + preference dividend + interest}}$$

For this purpose, cash flow would include only operating cash flow (ignoring investing cash flow & financing cash flow). As a point of the stress testing scale, a reduction of a certain percentage in income/sales with a simultaneous increase in expenses (for example, direct costs, etc) may result in charge (reduction) in cash flow. There is no minimum or maximum. The stress percentage depends on the industry, operating environment, and also the overall business environment at the time of analysis.

The above cluster is only indicative of the ratios that a commercial bank/financial institution may find useful from the credit risk evaluation angle. There may be other important ratios as well, such as:

- Finished goods holding.
- Cash flow interest coverage.
- Capital gearing ratio.
- Proprietory ratio.

Here's some wise advice from Rally & Brown: "You can envision a large number of potential financial ratios through which to examine almost every possible relationship. The trick is not to come up with more ratios but to attempt to limit the number of ratios so that you can examine them in a meaningful way." (*Investment Analysis and Portfolio Management*, 6th Edition, page 429.)

PRACTICAL IMPLICATIONS OF ACCOUNTING RATIOS IN CREDIT RISK EVALUATION

Accounting ratios are usually computed on the year-end position of assets, liabilities, profit/loss account components (over a position of generally 12 months) as reflected in the financial statements. This is based on a 'going concern' approach. However, one limitation here is that the 'static' view of assets & liabilities at the end of the year may not reflect the true and correct position. The alternative is to collect the figures from the party concerned, say, on a monthly basis (or as frequently as may be possible) and average the same on a 12-month basis. This may then, for credit risk evaluation purposes, be a more effective and dynamic tool. Irrespective of whether a bank/financial institution follows the year-end or average method of computation, the implications from the credit risk evaluation angle will depend upon:

- Adopting an appropriate credit rating system with generally

a large number of grades, where one of the inputs would be accounting ratios.
- The bank/financial institution will have to decide as a matter of corporate finance policy the nature of the accounting ratios to be used for credit risk evaluation (for example, there may be a different focus in assessing working capital for loans for fixed assets or for non-funded facilities/ investment in securities, etc.).
- Specific weights have to be allocated for accounting ratios (from the credit rating angle). Say, 20 out of a total of 100 points for the entire credit rating structure.
- The benchmarking for each ratio should be consistent with the bank's/financial institution's corporate finance policy.
- The maximum weightage for each component of the ratio should be fixed—say, 4 out of 20 points (20 being the total for all accounting ratios put together).
- Ratios conforming to the benchmark should be awarded the highest points. Those below the benchmark should be ranked with varying points, down to even zero.
- Total marks awarded for all adopted ratios should then be carried forward to the overall credit rating structure so as to arrive at final grade for each account/exposure.

In sum, accounting ratio is an inseparable arm of credit risk evaluation and its actual implications will depend upon the purpose, quantum and tenure of exposure on a case-by-case basis.

IS AN IDEAL RATIO AN INSURANCE AGAINST CREDIT RISK?

Although a powerful tool in credit risk evaluation, ratio analysis is not, however, the only criterion. There are a number of other parameters on which credit risk is analysed, like asset cover (credit mitigants as per Basel terminology), management quality of the borrowing party, macro-economic indicators that have an impact on the exposure, etc. Ratio analysis is not an insurance against credit risk because of the following:

- Each ratio is indicative of a certain aspect of the organisation. For example, current ratio is with respect to current assets and current liabilities only. It's not possible to look at the total picture from this.
- A favourable ratio may indicate poor performance on another dimension. For example a current ratio of over 2:1 (say 3:1) may show the management's inefficiency in holding current assets idle, with the accompanying carrying costs.
- Ratio analysis is an overwhelming reflection of past position. The same position may or may not hold in the future which is fraught with uncertainty especially where business is concerned.
- The computation of the ratio depends on the analyst's views, approach, perception and objectivity, particularly while identifying the components of a ratio. For example, while identifying current assets, some analysts may not consider certain assets as being 'current' (like inventory lying in stock beyond a particular period) or treat some liabilities as being 'current', although they may be classified as a term liability (like sundry unsecured loans without any specific repayment schedule).
- As far as ratio test is concerned, an analogy may be drawn with medical pathology. The blood report of an individual may show an ideal level of Haemoglobin on the date of the

test, which may drastically change soon after some adverse physiological developments. In the same way, ratio analysis may not provide any guarantee about the quality of credit assets on a continuous basis.

Keeping all these limitations in mind, it may be said that credit risk protection can come from a combination factors, and not from an isolated (ratio) one. Nevertheless, accounting ratios still play a dominant role in credit risk evaluation.

QUESTIONS

1. *A public sector bank has received an application from a newly registered small-scale industrial unit manufacturing plastic toys for the following credit facilities:*
   - *Term loan of Rs10 lakh with a repayment programme of 10 years.*
   - *Working capital advance of Rs3 lakh.*

   State which accounting ratios you will examine and how you would compare the ratios from the angle of trend analysis.

2. *An ideal ratio is only a broad indicator but not a continuing safeguard against risk. Explain.*

CHAPTER 6

The Credit Rating Mechanism

Rating implies an assessment or evaluation of a person, property, project or affairs against a specific yardstick/benchmark set for the purpose. In credit rating, the objective is to assess/evaluate a particular credit proposition (which includes investment) on the basis of certain parameters. The outcome indicates the degree of credit reliability and risk. These are classified into various grades according to the yardstick/benchmark set for each grade. Credit rating involves both quantitative and qualitative evaluations. While financial analysis covers the quantitative part, qualitative analysis covers a host of factors such as the firm's competitive strength within the industry/trade, likely effects on the firm's business of any major technological changes, regulatory/legal changes, etc., which are all 'management' factors.

The Basel Committee has defined credit rating as a 'summary indicator' of the risk inherent in individual credit, embodying an assessment of the risk of loss due to the default of a counter-party by considering relevant quantitative and qualitative information. Thus, credit rating is a tool for the measurement or quantification of credit risk.

WHO UNDERTAKES CREDIT RATING

There is no restriction on anyone rating another organisation as long as it serves their purpose. For instance, a would-be employee may like to do a rating before deciding to join a firm. Usually, however, credit rating is done by rating agencies and banks/ financial institutions.

Internationally, rating agencies like Standard & Poor's (S&P) and Moody's are well-known. In India, the four authorised rating agencies are CRISIL, ICRA, CARE, FITCH. They undertake rating exercises generally when an organisation wants to issue debt instruments like commercial paper, bonds, etc. Their ratings facilitate investor decisions, although normally they do not have any statutory/regulatory liability in respect of a rated instrument. This is because the rating is only an 'opinion' on the financial ability of an organisation to honour payments of principal and/or interest on a debt instrument, as and when they are due in the future. However, since the rating agencies have expertise in their field and are not tainted with any bias, their ratings are handy for market participants and regulatory authorities to form judgements on an instrument and/or the issuer and take decisions on them.

Banks/financial institutions do undertake structured rating exercises with quantitative and qualitative inputs to support a credit decision, whether it is sanction or rejection. However, they may be influenced by the rating—wherever available—of an instrument of a particular party by an external agency even though the purpose of a bank's credit rating may be an omnibus one—that is, to check a borrower's capacity and competence—while that of an external agency may be limited to a particular debt instrument.

UTILITY OF CREDIT RATING

In a developing country like India, the biggest source of funds for an organisation to acquire capital assets and/or for working capital requirements is the institutions, particularly commercial banks and development financial institutions. Hence, credit rating is one of the most important tools to measure, monitor and control credit risk, both at individual and portfolio levels. Overall, their utility may be viewed from the following angles:

- Credit selection/rejection.
- Evaluation of borrower in totality and of any particular exposure/facility.
- Transaction-level analysis and credit pricing and tenure.
- Activity-wise/sector-wise portfolio study keeping in view the macro-level position.
- Fixing outer limits for taking up/maintaining an exposure arising out of risk rating.
- Monitoring exposure already in the books and deciding exit strategies in appropriate cases.
- Allocation of risk capital for poor graded credits.
- Avoiding over-concentration of exposure in specific risk grades, which may not be of major concern at a particular point of time, but may in the future pose problems if the concentration continues.
- Clarity and consistency, together with transparency in rating a particular borrower/exposure, enabling a proper control mechanism to check risks associated in the exposure.

Basel-II has summed up the utility of credit rating in this way: "Internal risk ratings are an important tool in monitoring credit risk. Internal risk ratings should be adequate to support the identification and measurement of risk from all credit exposures and should be integrated into an institution's overall analysis of credit risk and capital adequacy. The ratings system should provide detailed ratings for all assets, not only for criticised or problem assets. Loan loss reserves should be included in the credit risk assessment for capital adequacy."

METHODS OF CREDIT RATING

1. **Through the cycle:** In this method of credit rating, the condition of the obligor and/or position of exposure is assessed assuming the 'worst point in the business cycle'. There may be a strong element of subjectivity on the evaluator's part while grading a particular case. It is also difficult to implement the method when the number of borrowers/exposures is large and varied.

2. **Point-in-time:** A rating scheme based on the 'current condition' of the borrower/exposure. The inputs for this method are provided by financial statements, current market position of the trade/business, corporate governance, overall management expertise, etc. Banks/financial institutions in India usually adopt the point-in-time method because:

- ➢ It is relatively simple to operate while at the same time providing a fair estimate of the risk grade of an obligor/ exposure.
- ➢ It can be applied consistently and objectively.
- ➢ Periodical review and downgrading are possible depending upon the position.

In the book *Risk Management* (McGraw-Hill, page 270), Michel Crouhy *et al*, while explaining the need for objectivity and methodology in credit rating had this to say: "The goal is to generate accurate and consistent risk ratings, yet also to allow professional judgement to significantly influence a rating where this is appropriate."

The point-in-time method fully serves the purpose of credit rating of a bank/financial institution.

SCORES/GRADES IN CREDIT RATING

The main aim of the credit rating system is the measurement or quantification of credit risk so as to specifically identify the probability of default (PD), exposure at default (EAD) and loss given default (LGD). Hence it needs a tool to implement the credit rating method (generally the point-in-time method). The agency also needs to design appropriate measures for various grades of credit at an individual level (a close analogy is the marks obtained by a student in various subjects and the final outcome in the form of ultimate grade achieved in the examination) or at a portfolio level. These grades may generally be any of the following forms:

i) Alphabet : AAA, AA, BBB, etc.
ii) Number : I, II, III, etc.

The fundamental reasons for various grades (as an outcome of aggregate scores) are as follows:

- Signalling default risks of an exposure.
- Facilitating comparison of risks to aid decision-making.
- Compliance with regulatory requirements of asset classification based on risks of exposures.
- Providing a flexible means to ultimately measure the credit risk of an exposure.

COMPONENTS OF SCORES/GRADES

Scores are mere numbers (1, 2 etc.) allotted for each quantitative and qualitative parameter—out of the maximum allowable for each parameter as may be fixed by an organisation—of an exposure. The issue of identification of specific parameters, its overall marks and finally relating aggregate marks (for all quantitative and qualitative parameters) to various grades is a matter of management policy and discretion—there is no statutory or regulatory compulsion. However, the management is usually guided in its efforts by the following factors:

- Size and complexity of operations.
- Varieties of its credit products and speed.
- The organisation's credit philosophy and credit appetite.
- Commitment of the top management to assume risks on a calculated basis without being risk-averse.

FUNDAMENTAL PRINCIPLE OF RATING AND GRADING

A basic requirement in risk grading is that it should reflect a clear and fine distinction between credit grades covering default risks and safe risks in the short run. While there is no 'ideal' number of grades that would facilitate achieving this objective, it is expected that 'more granularity' may serve the following purposes:

- Objective analysis of portfolio risk.
- Appropriate pricing of various risk grade borrowers, with a focus on low-risk borrowers in terms of lower pricing.
- Allocation of risk capital for high-risk graded exposures.
- Achieving accuracy and consistency.

According to the RBI, there should be an ideal balance (in numbers) between 'acceptable credit risk and unacceptable credit risk' in a grading system. It is suggested that:

- A rating scale may consist of 8-9 levels.
- Of the above, the first five levels may represent acceptable credit risks.
- The remaining four levels may represent unacceptable credit risks.

The above scales may be denoted by numbers (1, 2, 3 etc.) or alphabets (AAA, AA, BBB, etc). In deciding upon the number of scales/grades, the basic issue according to Michael Crouhy *et al* is: "Is the number of gradations appropriate to distinguish among the range of risks?"

SCOPE OF CREDIT RATING

While the need and utility of rating an exposure—fund-based/ non-funded credits and/or investment in securities—is now universally accepted, the exact scope of the rating methodology rests with individual organisations. The extent of the application of credit rating with scores and for eventual grading of an exposure may thus vary from organisation to organisation depending upon the nature of its business activity, size, extent of its operations, overall business policies, etc. As far as the banking industry is concerned, RBI guidelines (12 October 2002) *inter alia* state: "A bank can initiate the risk-grading activity on a relatively smaller/ narrower scale and introduce new categories as the risk gradation improves."

Credit rating may be undertaken on the basis of any of the following:

- Size of exposure. Say, an exposure of Rs 5 lakh and above (fund-based/non-fund-based).
- Tenure of exposure. Say, an exposure beyond one year (fund-based/non-fund-based).
- Complexion of the exposure. Say, an exposure to core industries, sensitive items like corporate shares, real & stock etc.
- Security/collateral-based exposure. Say, if an exposure is fully/substantially backed by tangible security/collateral, it may not face the same rigour of credit rating compared with unsecured/uncollateralised exposure.

The appreciation of any particular basis in the credit rating process will entirely be the prerogative of the organisation. In its guidelines on 12 October 2002, the RBI has recommended that banks rate all exposures. In order to be fully objective and consistent to derive the optimum benefits of the rating process, this advice may be useful for banks over a period of time.

TYPES OF CREDIT RATING

Generally speaking, credit rating is done for any type of exposure irrespective of the nature of an obligor's activities, status (government or non-government) etc. Broadly, however, credit rating done on the following types of exposures.

- Wholesale exposure: exposure to the commercial and institutional sector (C&I).

- Retail exposure: consumer lending, like housing finance, car finance, etc.

The parameters for rating the risks of wholesale and retail exposures are different. Here are some of them:

- In the wholesale sector, repayment is expected from the business for which the finance is being extended. But in the case of the retail sector, repayment is done from the monthly/periodical income of an individual from his salary/occupation.
- In the wholesale sector, apart from assets financed from bank funds, other business assets/personal assets of the owners may be available as security. In case of retail exposure, the assets that are financed generally constitute the sole security.
- Since wholesale exposure is for business purposes, enhancement lasts (especially for working capital finance) as long as the business operates. In the retail sector, however, exposure is limited to a point of time agreed to at the time of disbursement.
- 'Unit' exposure in the retail category is quite small generally compared to that of wholesale exposure.
- The frequency of credit rating in the case of wholesale exposure is generally annual, except in cases where more frequent (say half-yearly) rating is warranted due to certain specific reasons (for example, declining trend of asset quality). However, retail credit may be subjected to a lower frequency (say once in two years) of rating as long as exposure continues to be under the 'standard' asset category.

USUAL PARAMETERS FOR CREDIT RATING

A. Wholesale exposure: For wholesale exposures, which are generally meant for the business activities of the obligor, the following parameters are usually important:

Quantitative factors as on the last date of borrower's accounting year:

i. Growth in sales/main income.
ii. Growth in operating profit and net profit.
iii. Return on capital employed.
iv. Total debt-equity ratio.
v. Current ratio.
vi. Level of contingent liabilities.
vii. Speed of debt collection.
viii. Holding period of inventories/finished goods.
ix. Speed of payment to trade creditors.
x. Debt-service coverage ratio (DSCR).
xi. Cash flow DSCR.
xii. Stress test ratio (variance of cash flow/DSCR compared with the preceding year).

(Nos. x, xi and xii are usually taken into account for term exposures.)

Qualitative factors are adjuncts to the quantitative factors, although they cannot be measured accurately—only an objective opinion can be formed. Nevertheless, without assessing qualitative factors, credit rating would not be complete. These factors usually include:

i. How the particular business complies with the regulatory framework, standard and norms, if laid down.
ii. Experience of the top management in the various activities of the business.
iii. Whether there is any clear-cut succession plan for key personnel in the organisation.
iv. Initiatives shown by the top management in staying ahead of competitors.
v. Corporate governance initiative.
vi. Honouring financial commitments.
vii. Ensuring end-use of external funds
viii. Performance of affiliate concerns, if any.
ix. The organisation's ability to cope with any major technological, regulatory, legal changes etc.
x. Cyclical factors, if any, in the business and how they were handled by the management in the past year—macro-level industry/trade analysis.
xi. Product characteristics—scope for diversification.
xii. Approach to facing the threat of substitutes.

W. F. Treacy in *Credit Risk Rating* (1998) suggests looking at the following factors in the credit rating process for commercial lending:

- Industry/trade analysis at the macro level.
- Financial analysis.
- Quality of financial data.
- External returns.
- Analytical tools/models.
- Firm size/value.
- Management.

- Terms of facility.
- Other considerations.

B. Retail exposure: In undertaking credit rating for retail exposures—which consists mainly of lending for consumer durables and housing finance, or any other form of need-based financial requirements of individuals/groups in the form of educational loans—two vital issues need to be addressed:

i. Borrower's ability to service the loan.
ii. Borrower's willingness at any point of time to service the loan and/or to comply with the lender's requirement.

The parameters for rating retail exposures are an admixture of quantitative and qualitative factors. In both situations, the evaluator's objectivity in assessment is considered crucial for judging the quality of the exposure. The parameters may be grouped into four categories:

1. Personal details:

i. Age: economic life, productive years of life.
ii. Educational qualifications: probability of higher income and greater tendency to service and repay the loan.
iii. Marital status: greater need of a permanent settlement, lesser tendency to default.
iv. Number of dependents: impact on monthly outflow, reduced ability to repay.
v. Mobility of the individual, location: affects the borrower's repayment capacity and also his willingness to repay.

2. Employment details:

i. Employment status: income of the self-employed is not as stable as that of a salaried person.
ii. Designation: People at middle management and senior management levels tend to have higher income and stability.
iii. Gross monthly income, ability to repay.
iv. Number of years in current employment/business, stable income.

3. Financial details:

i. Margin/percentage of financing of borrowers: more the borrower's involvement, the less the amount of the loan.
ii. Details of borrower's assets: land & building, worth of the borrower or security.
iii. Details of a borrower's assets: bank balances and other securities, worth of the borrower or security.

4. Other details about the loan and borrower:

i. Presence and percentage of collateral—additional security.
ii. Presence of guarantor—additional security.
iii. Status symbols/lifestyle (telephone, television, refrigerator, washing machine, two-wheeler, car, cellular phone).
iv. Account relationship.

As per RBI guidelines, all exposures (without any cut-off limit) are to be rated.

MECHANISM OF CREDIT RATING

The quantitative and qualitative factors in the case of wholesale exposure and the four type factors in the case of the retail sector need to be accorded 'weights' or scores. The aggregate outcome will reflect the rating/grade of an exposure against a benchmark. Hence, the mechanism must lay down the following:

For wholesale exposure:

1. The marks for each parameter, with a range of marks for various ranges of a parameter, have to be fixed.

   If growth in the last completed year compared with the previous year is:

20% and above	:	4 marks
15% to less than 20%	:	3 marks
5% to less than 15%	:	2 marks
0% to less than 5%	:	1 mark
Negative growth	:	0 mark

   For qualitative factors also, there can be suitable scoring based on 'excellent position' (maximum marks) and lowest one 'non-satisfactory' (zero marks) may be fixed.

2. Aggregate marks for all the applicable parameters for each category may then be mapped into various grades taking the maximum marks as 100, as shown below.

3. Wherever a particular parameter is not applicable for an exposure, it may be ignored and aggregate marks be readjusted/graded accordingly.

Sl. No	Total Score for an Exposure	Grade Accorded	Implication of Grade Accorded
1.	86-100	AA+	Excellent Safety
2.	71-85	AA	Very Good Safety
3.	61-70	A	Good Safety
4.	51-60	BB+	Ordinary Safety
5.	41-50	BB	Less Ordinary Safety
6.	36-40	B	Low Safety
7.	31-35	C	Unsafe
8.	0-30	D	Loss Category

For retail exposure (consumer lending):

1. As with wholesale exposure, maximum marks for each parameter can be fixed. For example, age, months, income, etc.

2. Similarly, aggregate marks for each parameter can determine the overall grading of the account. While there may be eight grades in wholesale exposure because of the risk related issues in pricing involved, in the case of retail exposure, four/five grades are considered sufficient.

3. The scoring/grading systems in various banks/financial institutions may vary substantially depending on, *inter alia*, risk perceptions, thrust area and other allied factors.

CASE STUDIES

Commercial Loan Rating:

Beta Limited, a company incorporated under the Companies Act, is enjoying credit facilities from Mega Bank. The bank wants to have the account rated using its credit rating model. The rating model comprises subjective and objective parameters. The bank has dedicated, well-trained officers in its centralized credit analysis cell.

The company manufactures seamless pipes/tubes used in industrial applications. It has a substantial export business in Europe and some African countries. The export business accounts for a major portion of its total turnover and contributes significantly to its bottomline.

The top management comprises technocrats with very rich and varied experience of at least 20 years in manufacturing and project implementation. The company is controlled by the Miller group, which has a 26% shareholding in it, including the portion held by their close relatives. Reliable sources say there are some disputes regarding the sharing of property in the Miller family. It's most likely that the dispute has emerged due to the failure of a venture capital plan initiated by one of the brothers of the family. This involved substantial sums and could not take off due to the exit of the strategic partner from the venture at a crucial time. Also, Beta Ltd has no succession plan.

The financing banks (the company enjoys substantial credit facilities from the consortium) have objected to the deployment of funds without their prior permission for its expansion into an unrelated area—a mini cement plant, which is incurring huge cash losses due to its uneconomic size. The group is keeping its fingers crossed as to whether it should continue with this business or dispose it of, even at a discounted price.

Beta Ltd. has been constantly upgrading its systems with the latest technology available across the world to cut costs and improve efficiency. The business is banking on getting huge orders so that there is optimal utilisation of facilities. This way they can keep margins at the minimum and make competitive bids.

But there are problems. Competitors are quite aggressive. Another major area of concern is its urgent need for backward integration into solid rods. The company is facing a problem getting clearances (such as pollution due to certain chemical wastes discharged during the process) and certain control mechanisms have also to be put in place before seeking the necessary permission from the government for the expansion.

The company is ISO-certified and was given the 'Best Corporate Governance Practices' award last year by the Manufacturers' Association. The operating results of last two years were as under:-

OPERATING RESULTS	**31.3.01**	**31.3.02**
Sales	355.42	388.53
Cost of sales	314.91	351.24
Selling & administration cost	7.04	5.83
OPBDIT	33.47	31.46
Interest cost	16.47	15.25
Depreciation	1.62	1.56
Operating profit before tax	15.38	14.65
Net non-operating income	3.66	1.59
Profit before tax	19.04	16.24
Provision for tax	1.28	1.45
Net profit	17.76	14.79
Ratios		
Growth in sales		9.31%
Growth in OPBDIT		-6.01%
ROCE	14.14%	11.71%
Total debt equity ratio	2.04	1.83
Current ratio	1.42	1.49
Debtors collection period (days)	95	72
Inventory holding period (days)	63	62
Finished goods holding (days)	50	63
Creditors payment period (days)	60	55
Cash flow DSCR	2	2.2
Cash flow interest coverage	3	3.3
Stress test cash flow DSCR	1.8	1.92
Stress test cash flow interest coverage	2.78	3
Level of contingent liabilities (Cont Liab/TNW)	0.5	0.49

A	Objective Parameters	MARKS AWARDED BASED ON					Marks obtained
	Rating Parameter	**4**	**3**	**2**	**1**	**0**	
1	Growth in sales	>=20%	15-20%	5-15%	0-5%	Negative growth	2
2	Growth in operating profit (OPBDIT)	>=5%	4-5%	2-4%	0-2%	Negative growth	0
3	Return on capital employed (ROCE)	>=15%	11-15%	5-10%	0-5%	<=0%	3
4	Total debt – equity ratio	<=2.25	2.25 – 2.5	2.5 – 2.75	2.75 – 3	> 3 times	4
5	Current ratio	>=1.33	1.17 – 1.33	1 – 1.17	0.75 – 1	< 1 times	4
6	Level of continent liabilities (coverage)	<=0.5 times	0.5 – 0.70	0.7 – 0.85	0.85 – 1	>1	4
7	Debtors collection	<=45 days	45-75 days	75-100 days	100-120 days	>120 days	3
8	Inventory holding	<=45	45-60	60-75	75-100	>100 days	2
9	Finished goods holding	<=30	30-45	45-60	60-90	>90 days	1
10	Creditors Payment period	<20 days	20-30 days	30-50 days	50-75 days	> 75 days	1
11	Cash Flow DSCR	>=2.25	2-2.25	1.75-2.0	1.5-1.75	<1.5	3
12	Cash Flow Interest coverage	>=3.5	2.75-3.5	2.5-2.75	1.75-2.5	<1.75	3
13	Stress Tested CF DSCR	>=1.75	1.5-1.75	1.25-1.5	1-1.25	<1	4
14	Stress Tested CF Interest coverage	>=2.25	2-2.25	1.75-2	1.5-1.75	<1.5	4
							38

B	Subjective Parameters	MARKS AWARDED BASED ON					Marks obtained
	Rating Parameter	**4**	**3**	**2**	**1**	**0**	
1	Laid down regulatory framework, standard	If complied fully		Partially		Litigation/proceedings/non-compliance	2
2	Experience of top management	Very good (>15 yrs)	Good (10-15)	Moderate (5-10)	Little (0.5)	Nil	4
3	Succession plan for top management	Well planned		Adhoc		No Plan	0
4	Initiatives of management in new business areas	Success in initiatives		Certain problems/ delays but executed		No initiatives	2
5	Corporate governance	Well devised & executed		Moderate		No corporate governance	4
6	Honouring financial commitments	Timely		Delayed but honoured		Not honoured	4
7	End use of funds	Proper		Certain diversion with permission		Unauthorised diversion	0
8	Afiliate concerns' performance	Good		Average		NPA	2
9	Cyclical/seasonal factors	Low		Moderate		High	4
10	Characteristics of products of the company	Superior		Same as others		Inferior	2
11	Threat of substitutes	Very low / No threat		Moderate		High	2
							26

Module	No. of Parameters	Max. marks	Total Marks	Weight assigned	
A	14	4	56	60	
B	11	4	44	40	
	25		100	100	
	Marks obtained	**Max. marks**	**Weight**	**Net marks**	
A	38	56	60	40.71	
B	26	44	40	23.64	
				64	**'A' RATED ACCOUNT**
FINAL RATING					
86-100	**AA+**				
71-85	**AA**				
61-70	A				
51-60	BB+				
41-50	BB				
36-40	B				
31-35	C				
0-30	D				

HOUSING LOAN

Home Loan Rating:

Mr. A, an employee of a public sector undertaking since 1992 and currently serving as supervisor, has approached Amaron Bank for a housing loan of Rs 5 lakh repayable in 20 years. Mr. A has been banking with Deono Bank for the past 15 years and proposes to have a relationship with Amaron Bank. He is currently staying in a rented house. He has shifted houses four times in the past three years, which has now forced him to go in for his own house. He owns a two-wheeler, refrigerator, telephone and a television set. Details of other income are:

1. Gross annual salary - Rs 2,50,000
2. Annual deduction for LIC, PF, etc. - Rs 30,000
3. Stamp duty and instalments payable and eligible for tax deduction - Rs 20,000
4. Tax saving (eligible for rebate under sec.88) - Rs 25,000
5. Other monthly payments (EMIs) - Rs 1,000

His other personal details are:

1. Date of birth - 5th January 1968
2. Educational qualification - M.A. (Economics)
3. Marital status - Married
4. Dependants (excluding spouse) - Daughter & parents

The proposed house is a new one and is at a planning stage. The builder is considered very reliable, known for the quality of construction and timely completion of projects. The area in which the house is being constructed is slightly away from the market-place and the municipal authority is yet to provide necessary amenities like water, roads, etc. It appears that these would be provided within a few months. However, the area is developing fast and has lot of other new projects. It is estimated that a township would come into existence within a year or so, enhancing the pride and market value of the construction.

Equated monthly payment works out to Rs 4,825 (bank finances the borrower provided his total deductions do not exceed 60% of his income). Amaron Bank does not encourage granting loan for 'D' grade.

COMPUTATION – HOUSING LOAN	
Annual income	250000
Less : standard deduction	25000
Less: profession tax	2500
Income chargeable under salaries	222500
Deduction under chapter VI-A (interest on housing loan)	50000
Net taxable income	172500
Tax	25750
Tax saving (eligible investment up to Rs 70000/- @ 15%)	10500
Tax payable	15250
Other annual outflows (LIC, PF, tax saving, other EMIs)	67000
Total annual outflow (Tax+annual outflow+profession tax)	84750
Total permissible deduction (60% of Rs 2.50 lakh)	150000
Amount remaining for housing loan	65250
Maximum EMI payable by applicant per month	5437.50
% of actual EMI with maximum EMI	88.74%

	Housing Loan – Scoring	Awardable Scores				Borrower Scores
		4	2	1	0	
1	Age	21-40	40-45	45-50	Above 50	4
2	Educational qualification	Phd/PG	UG	HSC	<HSC	4
3	Marital status	Married	Single		Divorced	4
4	Location movement (Last 5 years)	No change		Changed once	Changed more than once	0
5	Dependants	Nil	One	Two	Over three	0
6	Employment	Salaried in Govt/PSU	Salaried Pvt/ Professional	Self employed	Others	4
7	Gross monthly income	Above 25000	20000-25000	10000-20000	<10000	2
8	Relationship with current employer	>7 yrs	5-7 yrs	3-5 yrs	<3 yrs	4
9	Designation	Executive	Managerial Supervisory	Officer	Junior/clerical	2
10	Actual EMI to Maximum EMI	<=60%	60-80%		>80%	0
11	Other assets as % to loan amount	>100%	75-100%		<75%	0
12	Quality of construction (existing) Building construction (New)	Very good	Good	Average	Poor	4
13	Availability of basic amenities	Very good	Good	Average	Poor	1
14	Saleability of the property	Very good	Good	Average	Poor	1
15	Bank's account holder	Yes			No	0
16	Age of building (existing property only)	<3 yrs	3-5 yrs	5-8 yrs	>8 yrs	

Housing Loan – Scoring		Awardable Scores				Borrower Scores
		4	**2**	**1**	**0**	
17	Stage of construction (new property only)	Final/ complete	Work in progress	Foundation	Planning	0
18	Guarantor presence	Yes			No	0
19	Lifestyle (0,5 mark for each yes and 0 for no) – 4 marks maximum Car, scooter, fridge, telephone, mobile, TV, microwave oven etc.)					2
	FINAL SCORING					**32**
	A	**60-76**				
	B	**40-59**				
	C	**20-39**		**FINAL GRADE**	**'C'**	
	D	**0-19**				

CAR LOAN

Car Loan Rating:

Mr. S.S. Rao, a Senior Engineer in a private sector company manufacturing electrical products, has approached Amaron Bank for a car loan. He joined the company as a trainee when he was 23 years old. He has had an account relationship with the bank for the past 10 years. He wants to purchase a new Hyundai Santro car costing Rs 4.25 lakh. He will put up the required margin amount of Rs 85,000 (20% of the outlay) from his personal savings. He wants to repay the loan within three years (see Note below). His income and other details are:

1. Gross annual salary - Rs 4,00,000
2. Annual deduction for LIC, PF, etc. - Rs 70,000
3. Tax saving (eligible for rebate under sec.88) - Rs 30,000
4. Other monthly payments (EMIs) - Nil

His other personal details are:

1. Date of birth - 25th March 1960
2. Educational qualification - M.E. (Elec. Engg.)
3. Marital status - Married
4. Dependants (excluding spouse) - Two sons

He owns a house (ancestral property) worth Rs 10 lakh where he lives with his family. He also has sundry assets: farmland and a tractor worth Rs 4 lakh. However, he has had no income from agriculture during the past two-three years. Last year he had done some construction work on the property for which he obtained a loan of Rs 5 lakh from his employer with a repayment period of 15 years. The interest payments on the loan work out to Rs 49,000 (at 10%) per year. There are no other charges on his properties, but he has not extended any property as collateral. He has a refrigerator, cellphone, television and washing machine.

Note:

As per his requirement of repayment over three years, the EMI works out to Rs 10,970. However, it may be suggested to the borrower to go in for a repayment period of, say, six years where the EMI works out to Rs 6,299. He may also avail the loan for over six years up to the maximum period for which a car loan is extended by the bank (maximum of eight years in the case of Amaron Bank for an entry-level model and 15 years for the luxury segment). A suitable option—say six or seven years— may be suggested for the borrower and the scoring reworked accordingly. The computation of scoring is done based on repayment in six years.

The EMI for the car loan works out to Rs 6,299 for six years and Rs 10,970 for three years. **(The bank finances the borrower provided his total deductions do not exceed 60% of his income). Amaron Bank considers loan for A, B & C grades.**

COMPUTATION – CAR LOAN	
Annual income	400000
Less : Standard deduction	20000
Less: Profession tax	2500
Income chargeable under salaries	377500
Deduction under chapter VI-A (interest on loan)	49000
Net taxable income	328500
Tax	72550
Tax saving (eligible investment up to Rs 100000/- @ 15%)	15000
Tax payable	57550
Other annual outflows (LIC, PF, tax saving)	100000
Total annual outflow (Tax+annual outflow+profession tax)	160050
Total permissible deduction (60% of Rs 4 lakh)	240000
Amount remaining for car loan	79950
Maximum EMI payable by applicant per month	6662.50
% of actual EMI with maximum EMI	94.54%

Car Loan – Scoring		Awardable Scores				Borrower Scores
		4	2	1	0	
1	Age	21-40	40-45	45-50	Above 50	2
2	Educational qualification	Phd/PG	UG	HSC	<HSC	4
3	Marital status	Married	Single		Divorced	4
4	Location movement (Last 5 years)	No change		Changed once	Changed more than once	4
5	Dependants	Nil	One	Two	Over three	1
6	Employment	Salaried in Govt/PSU	Salaried Pvt/ Professional	Self employed	Others	2
7	Gross monthly income	Above 25000	20000-25000	10000-20000	<10000	4
8	Relationship with current employer	>7 yrs	5-7 yrs	3-5 yrs	<3 yrs	4
9	Designation	Executive	Managerial Supervisory	Officer	Junior/clerical	4
10	Actual EMI to Maximum EMI	<=60%	60-80%		>80%	0
11	Margin	>60%	40-60%		<40%	0
12	Other Assets as % to Loan Amt	>100%	75-100%	Average	<75%	4
13	Collateral provided	>50%	<50%	Average	Nil	0
14	Type of vehicle	New	1-3 yrs	3-5 yrs	>5 yrs	4
15	Resale value of car	Good		Average	Poor	1
16	Bank's account holder	Yes			No	4

Car Loan – Scoring		Awardable Scores				Borrower Scores
		4	**2**	**1**	**0**	
17	Guarantor presence	Yes			No	0
18	Lifestyle (0,5 mark for each Yes and 0 for No) – 4 marks maximum Car, scooter, fridge, telephone, mobile, computer, washing machine, TV, microwave oven etc.)					2
	FINAL SCORING					**44**
	A	**60-76**				
	B	**40-59**		**FINAL GRADE**	**'B'**	
	C	**20-39**				
	D	**0-19**				

QUESTIONS

1. *Define credit rating and state its utility from the credit risk management angle.*

2. *The 'point-in-time' method of credit rating is more objective. Elucidate.*

3. *Mr Sunil Tendulkar is working in a multinational corporation in Mumbai as a sales representative. His other particulars are as under:*

   - *Monthly take-home pay : Rs 20,000/-*
   - *He does not currently have any monthly commitments towards repaying any loan.*
   - *He has been staying with his family (which includes himself, his wife and a young son) in rented premises for the past five years.*
   - *He is an MBA (marketing).*
   - *He approaches Good Bank Ltd for a home loan of Rs 10 lakh for purchasing a flat. You are engaged by the bank to devise an appropriate credit rating for a home loan. Which can you highlight for taking care of Tendulkar's loan application?*

4. *Credit rating for a business loan is more extensive than that for a retail loan. Why?*

CHAPTER 7

The Credit Risk Model

A credit risk model is a quantitative study of credit risk, covering both good borrowers and bad borrowers. According to Anthony Saunders *et al*, a credit risk model is a mathematical model containing the loan applicant's characteristics either to calculate a score representing the applicant's probability of default or to sort borrowers into different default risk classes (*Financial Institutions and Management*, McGraw-Hill Publications, 4th Edition, page 277). A model is considered effective if a suitable 'validation' process is also built in with adequate power and calibration. As a matter of fact, a model without the necessary and appropriate validation is only a hypothesis.

UTILITY

Banks and financial institutions in particular may derive the following benefits if they install an appropriate credit risk model:

- It will enable them to compute the 'present value' of a loan asset or fixed income security, taking into account the organisation's past experience and assessment of the future scenario.
- It facilitates the measurement of credit risk in quantitative terms, especially in cases where promised cash flows may not materialise.
- It would enable an organisation to compute its regulatory capital requirement based on an internal ratings approach.
- An appropriate credit risk model will facilitate an impact study of credit derivatives and loan sales/securitisation initiatives.
- It facilitates the pricing of loans and provides a competitive edge to the players.

- ➢ It helps the top management in an organisation in financial planning, customer profitability analysis, portfolio management, and capital structuring/restructuring, managing risk across the geographical and product segments of the enterprise.
- ➢ Regulatory authorities find it easier to evaluate banks/financial institutions that have a suitable credit risk model in place.
- ➢ Above all, a credit risk model enables achieving the objectives of what to measure, how to measure and how to interpret the results.

DISTINCTION BETWEEN CREDIT RATING AND CREDIT RISK MODEL

Both credit rating and a credit risk model serve the common purpose of evaluating the quality of an exposure. However, from the risk management angle, there is a subtle distinction between the two:

Credit rating	Credit risk model
➢ Applies to all types of exposures so as to identify high quality, medium quality, low quality and poor quality exposures using a benchmark process.	➢ Applies predominantly to low and poor quality exposures to ascertain 'present value', especially in cases where the promised cash flow may not materialise.
➢ Focus is mainly on the 'probability of repayment'.	➢ Focus is mainly on the 'probability of default'.
➢ Financial parameters and state of exposures over a short period— usually of one year— form the core of the credit rating exercise.	➢ Sophisticated statistical techniques like linear and multiple discriminant analysis, etc. are used as tools for analysis over the long term.

Credit rating	Credit risk model
➢ Facilitates grading exposures to an ideal range of 8-9 grades comprising both of 'good' and 'bad' exposures.	➢ Facilitates computation of 'exposure of default', 'probability of default', 'loss given default' towards risk capital requirement.

CREDIT RISK MANAGEMENT TECHNIQUES

Techniques are methods to accomplish a desired aim. In credit risk modelling, the aim is essentially to compute the probability of default of an asset/loan. Broadly, the following range is available to an organisation going in for a credit risk model:

- Econometric technique: statistical models such as linear probability and logit model, linear discriminant model, RARUC model, etc.
- Neural networks: computer-based systems using economic techniques on an alternative implementation basis.
- Optimisation model: mathematical process of identifying optimum weights of borrower and loan assets.
- Hybrid system: Simulation by direct casual relationship of the parameters.

FOCAL POINTS OF APPLICATION OF MODELS

- In all lending decisions, especially in the retail lending segment, models are very useful since in the ordinary course of the lending business, the probability of default has an overriding implication on credit appraisal decisions.
- It acts as an instrument to validate (or invalidate) the credit rating process in an organisation.

- It's possible to work out reasonably the quantum of risk premium that is loaded in pricing credit with the backing of an appropriate credit risk model.
- Credit risk models help in diagnosing potential problems in a credit/allied business proposition and at the same time facilitate prompt corrective action.
- In the securitisation process, credit risk models enable the construction of a pool of assets that may be acceptable to investors.
- Appropriate strategies can be designed to monitor borrowal accounts with the aid of credit risk models.

PREREQUISITES FOR ADOPTING A MODEL

The adoption of any statistical/mathematical model by an organisation depends upon the company's size and complexity of operations, risk-bearing capacity, risk appetite, overall risk evaluation and the control environment. However, while adopting any particular form of the credit risk model, the following prerequisites should be satisfied:

- A wide range of historical data should be used.
- There must be assistance from a compact Management Information System (MIS).
- The data must be reliable and authentic.
- All the significant risk elements depending upon the organisation's range of activities must be built into the model.
- The model's assumptions must be realistic.
- The model should be capable of differentiating the element and intensity of risk in various categories of exposures.
- The model should be in a position to identify over-

concentration—hence higher-order risk—in the portfolio.

- The model should provide clear signals of incipient sickness and problems in exposures.
- It should facilitate working out adequacy/inadequacy in the provisions for non-performing exposures.
- It should have room for making impact analysis of macro situations on various exposures of the organisation.
- It should be in a position to help the management determine the likely effect on profitability of the various risk contents in the exposures.
- There should be periodical validation of the model.
- There should be an ongoing system of review for the model to judge its efficacy.

QUESTIONS

1. *Define credit risk model. Distinguish between credit rating and credit risk model.*

2. *What are the essential requirements for adopting any credit risk model?*

CHAPTER 8

Credit Risk Portfolio Management

1. Objectives of Credit Risk Portfolio Management
2. Advantages of Credit Risk Portfolio Management
3. Basic principles of Credit Risk Portfolio Management
4. Basic attributes of Credit Risk Portfolio Management
5. Constraints in Portfolio Management
6. Credit Paradox
7. Techniques of Portfolio Credit Risk Control
8. How Industry/Sectoral Analysis is Conducted
9. Brief specimen of Industry/Sectoral Report
10. Questions

DEFINITION

Banks, financial institutions and other organisations extend credit to individual borrowers. The lending/extension of credit may stretch to a number of borrowers who may have a common linkage. This linkage may be the result of:

- Involvement in the same trade/business.
- Located in the same geographical setting or in close proximity.
- Common owners/management.

A credit portfolio therefore consists of individual borrowers in a pool who are connected to each other in some way or the other. From the viewpoint of enterprise-wide risk management, credit risk portfolio management is the process of identification, measurement, monitoring and control of concentration risk arising out of the common link between the borrowers—whether technical, economic, financial or in any other business manner.

OBJECTIVES OF CREDIT RISK PORTFOLIO MANAGEMENT

- To identify, measure, monitor and control not only expected losses from each credit transaction but also unexpected losses from the entire portfolio.
- To achieve an 'optimum portfolio', with the lowest risk content for a given level of income or the highest income with a specified risk content.
- To obtain the maximum benefit of diversification and to reduce likely losses owing to credit concentration to parties with some form of common linkage.

- To act as a refined substitute to the forward-looking approach inherent in the asset/exposure relationship by providing wide-ranging inputs of correlation and volatility.
- To reduce, if not eliminate, the risks of unexpected happenings to a portfolio because of the occurrence of events arising out of the linkage—like being in the same industry/trade, same owner/management, etc.
- To facilitate credit decisions and risk-mitigating steps in an integrated manner keeping in view the intimate relationship in a credit portfolio of correlation and volatility.

ADVANTAGES OF CREDIT RISK PORTFOLIO MANAGEMENT

- It is rightly said that defaults and credit migration (both upward & downward) are directly linked to the macroeconomic situation. Credit cycles move in tandem with business cycles in an economy. A credit portfolio study brings out the actual situation on an ongoing basis, enabling the management to initiate risk-mitigating actions quickly.
- Portfolio management enables the measurement of credit concentration risk in any dimension having a direct effect on one or the other. For example, industry/trade grouping, locational closeness, country risk and instrument-based relationship.
- A systematic approach to portfolio analysis enables the diversification of risk exposures, going by the age-old principle of 'All eggs should not be put in the same basket'.
- A clear-cut and rational capital allocation process is possible by ensuring regular analysis of diversification benefits and concentration risks. Risk increases with a decline in credit

quality and goes down with an improvement in credit quality.

- Credit derivatives can be managed better with portfolio management because their risk contents are more intensified and have a more crucial effect on an organisation.
- More rational pricing of credit exposure is possible when an organisation has an appropriate credit risk management system in place.

BASIC PRINCIPLES OF CREDIT RISK PORTFOLIO MANAGEMENT

- Individual borrower/exposure level is the foundation of the portfolio study.
- A framework is to be designed (depending on the size and complexity of the organisation) in which there is aggregation of all credit risk exposures and ways and means to compare products and sectoral risks.
- A system to measure various types of credit exposures should be put in place keeping in view the element of correlation and volatility.

BASIC ATTRIBUTES OF CREDIT RISK PORTFOLIO MANAGEMENT

According to the Reserve Bank of India (in its guidelines dated 12 October 2002) portfolio credit risk measurement and management depends on two key attributes: correlation and volatility.

Correlation indicates a relation between two or more things, implying an intimate or necessary connection. These may be mathematical, statistical or any other variables that tend to be associated or occur together in an unexpected way. In other words, if there is interdependence between two or more variable quantities in such a manner that a change in the value of one results in a change in the value or expectation of the other, then they are said to be correlated from a statistical angle. The RBI guidelines *inter alia* state: "Credit portfolio correlation would mean number of times companies/counter-parties in a portfolio defaulted simultaneously. Volatility, on the other hand, means rapid or unexpected change which may be difficult to capture or hold permanently."

The main purpose of portfolio management would be to examine the correlation between the defaulting of a pool of exposure (portfolio) to the volatility of a particular industry/sector activity. This is done so as to measure and manage the non-diversifiable risk in a portfolio as distinguished from diversifiable risk. A low default correlation would mean that non-diversifiable risk content in a portfolio has little significance. A high default correlation, on the other hand, means more risk.

The implication of correlation and volatility in a portfolio study has been succinctly explained by the RBI guidelines: "Consider two companies, one operates large capacities in the steel sector and the other a large player in the cement sector, promoted by two entirely unrelated promoters. Though these would classify as two separate counter-parties, both of them may be highly sensitive to the Government's expenditure in new projects/investments. Thus, reduction in Government investments could impact these two companies simultaneously (correlation), impacting the credit-quality of such a portfolio (volatility), even though from a regulatory or conventional perspective, the risk had been diversified (two separate promoters, two separate industries). Thus, though the credit portfolio may be well-diversified and fulfils the prescribed criteria for counter-party exposure limits, the high correlation in potential performance between two counter-parties may impact the portfolio quality (default levels) under stress conditions."

CONSTRAINTS IN PORTFOLIO MANAGEMENT

Though credit risk portfolio management—with the aid of concepts like correlation and volatility—is very useful, it does suffer from some constraints. Here are some:

- There are a number of variables like correlation of returns, correlation of factors explaining returns, correlation of default probability, correlation of rating category, correlation of spreads, etc. Depending upon the size, complexity and coverage of the portfolio, it has to be decided which of these variables need to be considered, and is a constraint in computing the coefficient of correlation.
- Distribution of returns contains 'fat tails' which may indicate that, in the region of loan loss, the probability is more than that dictated by the normal distribution curve.
- A multi-period model to address the issue of transaction costs in credit risk needs to be put in place as against the easy solution of the single period approach.
- The absence of price discovery in a portfolio of debt securitisation taking into account seniority, covenants, call options, etc. poses problems.
- Data limitation, with the focus on geography and industry identification, reduces the efficacy of portfolio management.

(*Managing Credit Risk: The Next Great Financial Challenge*, Caoutte *et al*, 1998).

CREDIT PARADOX

The attributes of correlation and volatility in portfolio management facilitate diversification of credit risks. But often in the process a paradox emerges: whether to expand a particular portfolio with a higher order of risk but with lower transaction costs and/or higher spreads or be content with low-risk and low-earning exposures. Furthermore, increasing exposure to the same party/group that is known to an organisation for a long time and provides a good source of income may apparently be in its interests but may lead to concentration risks. This in turn may lead to unexpected losses. This kind of situation is called a 'credit paradox' (*Internal Credit Risk Model*, Michael K., 1999).

TECHNIQUES OF PORTFOLIO CREDIT RISK CONTROL

Any effort at credit risk control—be it at the individual credit or portfolio levels—has the following main ingredients.

- Expected and unexpected losses are estimated on a consistent basis with reliable data back-up.
- There must be a balance between income and risk level.
- Adequate safety nets must be built in should estimates and actuals at any time widely vary, putting the organisation in peril.

The following two techniques aimed at controlling exposure at the portfolio level may be adopted simultaneously but not in isolation:

1. **Group exposure ceilings:** The RBI has prescribed that

banks/financial institutions limit their exposures—both funded and non-funded—to a certain portion of their capital fund. This is applicable for both single exposure and group exposure. From the viewpoint of portfolio exposure control, the prevailing guideline suggests that a bank/financial institution must place a ceiling on group exposure (beyond which no group exposure can be taken up without the RBI's prior approval). The ceilings are:

- Single exposure: ceiling of 15% of the bank's capital fund (additional 5% in the case of infrastructure exposure).
- Group exposure: ceiling of 40% of the bank's capital fund (additional 5% for infrastructure exposure).

This technique aims at portfolio control, at both the individual and group (i.e., borrowers interlinked through shareholding, commonality of management, etc.) levels. As a result of correlating the overall single/group exposure ceiling with its capital fund, a bank ensures—from the credit risk angle—that its own stake in an unexpected situation does not go out of gear.

This mechanism may be treated as 'risk limits'.

2. **Industry/sectoral ceiling:** Alongside the above measure, it may be useful to have an industry/sectoral ceiling as part of portfolio management. In this respect, a bank/financial institution (or any other organisation extending a credit facility) may follow these rules:

   - Fix an absolute amount as a ceiling for a particular

industry (like textiles, pharmaceuticals etc) or sector (real estate etc.).

- In so doing, the organisation may go by the position of a particular industry/sector from time to time. It may also be necessary to have a ceiling based on the location of the industry/sector. For example, if a particular place/state is considered unsuitable for a particular line of activity, it should be kept in view while examining the exposure ceiling.
- Industry/sectoral analysis/study should not be a one-time affair but be on an ongoing basis. The feedback from such analysis/study will determine the ceiling desired for a particular industry/sector.

CONDUCTING INDUSTRY/SECTORAL ANALYSIS

This type of analysis/study is best performed by experts like technocrats and economists. There are organisations in India that do such studies and sell their reports. CRIS-INFAC (a CRISIL concern), ICRA, CARE and CMIE have skilled staff who prepare their reports on a continuing basis based on market survey and inputs from various sources. Generally, the following aspects have to be taken into account while preparing industry/sectoral reports:

- Overall position of the domestic economy as per GDP growth.
- Overall consumption growth—domestic and overseas.
- A particular industry/sector's position in the economy as a whole.
- Effect of government policies on the industry/sector.
- Availability of inputs—raw materials, labour, power, transportation etc.

- Scope for diversification.
- Demand-supply gap.
- Possibility of threats from substitutes/new parties.
- Significant factors like cyclicality and seasonality.
- Industry sector financials in terms of return on capital employed (ROCE), operating profit growth, debt-equity ratio, current ratio etc.
- Capacity utilisation.
- Raw material consumption in relation to sales.
- Average debtors collection in relation to sales.
- Average creditors payment in relation to purchases.
- Average inventory holding.

BRIEF SPECIMEN OF INDUSTRY/SECTORAL REPORT

While the structure and content of report may vary from industry to industry according to the purpose for which the analysis/study is undertaken, a brief specimen report on the **food processing industry** is presented below for credit risk portfolio monitoring purposes.

Introduction

The food processing sector consists of the following sectors:

- Foodgrains.
- Milk products.
- Fruits.
- Vegetables.
- Other agro-based items.

The activity involves low capital expenditure and the requirement of technical knowledge and expertise is fairly small.

Production process: Depending on the end-product, the production process may be of the following types:

- Primary processing.
- Secondary processing.
- Tertiary processing.

Primary processing covers cleaning, powdering and refining agricultural produce. Secondary processing is a value-addition process such as making tomato puree, processing meat products etc. Tertiary processing on the other hand covers food items that have gone through the tertiary process and are ready for consumption at the point of sale, like bakery products, jams, sauces etc.

Characteristics of the food processing business

- Fragmented, with various small units as against the global situation of massive scales of operation.
- High levels of wastage.
- Low farm yield mainly due to the lack of modernisation of agricultural methods.
- High employment potential (it is estimated that an investment of Rs 100 crore creates around 54,000 jobs as compared to 25,000 in a mass consumption item like paper).

Major constraints

- Inadequate infrastructure. The food processing industry deals in items that are very perishable. Lack of dependable storage and transportation facilities hinders its growth.
- Laws/directives on prevention of food adulteration are not sufficiently stringent.

Demand and supply position

It is reported that the Indian food processing market is worth around Rs 25,000 crore. In view of the perishable nature of the items, the industry concentrates on local operations. With a growing population, the industry has high growth potential.

Company	Products
Hindustan Lever Limited	Ice creams, packaged wheat flour, salt, tea, bread, oils, fats and dairy products.
Haldirams	Snack food, traditional Indian sweets.
MTR Foods	Convenience food, ice creams, snack food.
Cadbury India	Chocolates, sugar confectionery, malt drinks.
Ruchi Group	Soya products, palmolein oil, sunflower oil, hydrogenated vegetable fat and oil.
Dabur	Fruit juices, cooking paste and sauces.
GlaxoSmithKline	Malt drinks
Gujarat Co-operative Milk Marketing Federation	Ice creams, butter, cheese, milk powder, traditional Indian sweets, chocolates.

Company	Products
Godrej Foods	Fruit juices, tomato puree, nuts, groundnut oil, refined palmolein oil and hydrogenated oil.
Pepsi Foods India	Soft drinks but also large consumer of tomatoes and chillies for preparing pastes for exports.
Britannia Industries	Biscuits, milk products like cheese and butter
Parle Foods	Biscuits and other related products
Mother Dairy	Ice creams, butter, cheese, milk powder, traditional Indian sweets, chocolates.
Venkateshwara Hatcheries	Frozen chicken
Nestle India	Chocolates, sugar confectionery, malt drinks, milk powder.

Export scenario

Processed food accounts for around 25% of our country's total agro exports. Fruits, spices, vegetables, rice and various animal products are the main items exported.

Government policy/controls

- No industrial licence is generally necessary for food processing. However, a licence is needed for industries engaged in beer, potable alcohol, wines, cane sugar, hydrogenated animal fats and oils.

- Obtaining ISI mark is relatively easy and carries a good value in branded processed items.

Important overall information base of the food processing industry

• Return on capital employed	:	38.44%
• Operating profit growth	:	9.43%
• Debt-equity Ratio	:	0.4 : 1
• Current ratio	:	1.5 : 1
• Capacity utilisation	:	Low
• Raw material consumption	:	70% of sales
• Average debtors collection	:	25 days
• Average creditors payment	:	61 days
• Average inventory holding period	:	22 days

Conclusion

The food processing industry in India has ample opportunities for growth—nationally and internationally. The industry has the unique advantage of low capital investment, lower gestation periods and operating cycles and, to top it all, an industry-friendly environment from the regulatory point of view. At the same time, it has the potential to enhance agricultural activity and employment.

In sum, the growth of this industry needs to be encouraged with, however, a provision for an ongoing review mechanism.

QUESTIONS

1. *What is common linkage in a credit portfolio? What are the advantages of systematic credit risk portfolio management? Are there any constraints?*

2. *State the various techniques in the portfolio credit control system.*

3. *You have been engaged by Good Bank Ltd., to prepare an industry analysis report on the tyre industry. State the main points you would cover in your report.*

CHAPTER 9

Off-Balance Sheet Exposures: Management and Risk Quantification

1. Exposure Control Mechanism
2. Monitoring Control
3. Risk Mapping
4. Credit Risk Mitigants
5. Risk Rating with Transition Matrix
6. Questions

From the credit risk angle, how different is a non-funded off-balance sheet exposure from a funded exposure?

Funded exposures are 'on balance sheet' items, comprising loans & advances and investments. In such cases, as there is an outgo of cash/cash equivalent, from the risk perspective it would have a direct impact on the balance sheet. On the other hand, though off-balance sheet items are non-funded exposures (letters of credit, guarantees, derivatives etc.) there is always the possibility of materialising the commitments should there be any breach and/or non-compliance by the parties on whose behalf such commitments have been made. If that happens, such exposures would be listed in the balance sheet on a par with funded exposures. Hence, for all practical purposes, off-balance sheet exposures are treated in the same manner as funded exposures in modern banking, where credit risk is widely prevalent and the corporate life span is shorter (some management experts are of the opinion that generally corporate life expectancy is around 30 years, while human life expectancy is on an average around 70 years across the world). From the regulatory point of view, off-balance sheet exposures are now clubbed with funded exposures. Therefore, from the credit risk angle, it makes no distinction between a funded exposure and a non-funded exposure as an off-balance sheet item.

EXPOSURE CONTROL MECHANISM

As explained in previous chapters, the RBI has prescribed single exposure/group exposure ceilings for banks/financial institutions as a percentage of their capital fund.

As far as off-balance sheet exposures are concerned, the

following directives came into force with effect from 1 April 2003:

- All off-balance sheet exposures (instead of the 50% fixed earlier) are to be treated as exposure, thereby removing the distinction between non-funded and funded exposures.
- In determining single/group exposure ceiling, forward contracts in foreign exchange and other derivative products—swaps, options etc.—are to be reckoned at their replacement value.

It is now internationally acknowledged that a credit risk management system must place equal emphasis on funded and non-funded exposures to ensure a healthy portfolio of exposures.

MONITORING/CONTROL

Besides exercising overall control of exposures at the portfolio level, the following issues are important in monitoring/controlling off-balance sheet exposure.

- With respect to off-balance sheet exposures operative beyond a one-year period (like guarantees, LCs for fixed assets/projects), a thorough viability study—like that done for term loans—should be done.
- An ongoing control mechanism tracking the progress of the projects on which exposures are made should be in place. In the case of guarantees/LCs issued for the acquisition/installation of capital assets, it must be ensured that the project is in line with the terms and conditions covering the contract/LC/guarantee terms.
- Since no financial outlay is envisaged in off-balance sheet

exposure and the earnings stem from the paper commitments only, the temptation to undertake such exposures without appropriate evaluation (which should be on a par with evaluation of funded exposures) for the sake of obtaining 'fee-based income' should be avoided.

- In larger banks/financial institutions that have sizable off-balance sheet exposures, a cadre of officials specialising in evaluating/monitoring such exposures should be developed as a long-term measure, to ensure a safe and sound system.

CREDIT RISK QUANTIFICATION

Risk mapping: 'Risk' as defined in the first chapter appears to contain an element of 'notional view', as the eventual outcome of a risk proposition is a mere 'possibility'. In that respect an accurate quantification of credit risk is not possible. Quantitative/statistical models/tools only facilitate an objective assessment of inherent risk volume so that necessary checks and balances are in place. Risk mapping, risk mitigants and risk rating with transition matrix are known drivers in credit risk management, including quantification of credit risk.

Credit risk covers the risks arising from funded and non-funded exposures, including derivative transactions. A bank/financial institution or any organisation undertaking any type of credit risk transaction is required to map out or survey the entire gamut of its risk transactions in the order of their magnitude. With this exercise, it would be possible to work out an appropriate plan of action. Depending on the size, complexity and area of operation, an organisation should map its credit risks. For example, if an organisation operates mainly in a politically or socially disturbed area (like Gujarat and Kashmir in India) the mapping of its credit risk with the aid of credit rating may not be the same as that of other organisations in more peaceful areas. Furthermore, a commercial bank's risk mapping of project loans/terms may not match with that of development banks like IDBI or IFCI.

Michael Crouhy *et al* aptly state the utility of risk mapping in the book *Risk Management* (page 624): "After the objectives have been set, and the general nature of the risks to be managed is decided upon, it is essential to map the relevant risks to ESTIMATE THEIR CURRENT AND FUTURE MAGNITUDES."

In the credit risk mapping exercise, it is necessary to identify risks that can be insured/mitigated in any manner to reduce the magnitude of any adverse impact, current and future.

Mitigants of credit risk: Any credit proposition carries with it a certain risk of loss—whatever be the level of perfection at the initial evaluation stage. But it is obvious that the name of the game is business. Hence what is required is ways and means to reduce the severity of the effect should a transaction involve a credit loss.

The Basel Committee considers the following as being effective credit risk mitigants:

- Collateral (tangible, marketable) securities.
- Guarantees (for institutional guarantees it is recognised that the same meets a threshold external credit rating).
- Credit derivatives.

The extent to which a particular credit risk mitigant helps depends on the quantum of exposure, or the strength of the mitigant.

Risk rating with transition matrix: Based on internal credit rating modules (as explained in earlier chapters), an institution may develop a transition matrix for various credit risk exposures at the portfolio level every year. This matrix (frequency distribution) tracks upward/downward credit migration and reveals the extent of volatility in the exposures, especially the downward migration on the credit rating scale. From this exercise it is possible to identify how many exposures have been downgraded over a one-year horizon and how many have improved. Depending on the severity of the downgraded exposures, action points may be quickly drawn up to make improvements. A transition matrix hence facilitates the monitoring/control of credit risks in a larger way.

Broadly, a transition matrix may operate in the following manner:

- Mean (probability) transition matrix and standard deviation matrix are worked out.
- The matrix will then throw up signals on exposures, with ratings migrating upward/downward.
- Probability of default (the likelihood of default over a given time horizon), loss given default (the proportion of the likely loss of exposure if default occurs) and exposure *at* default (the amount of the facility that is likely to be drawn if a default occurs) may be drawn up.

For this exercise to be useful, an ongoing system of review must be installed with a focus on initiating prompt remedial actions wherever necessary, including the crystallisation of credit risk mitigants wherever available.

The transition matrix is handy in computing economic capital which by itself acts as a shock absorber for an institution under the risk management system. This aspect is being considered by the Basel Committee.

QUESTIONS

1. *Do you agree with the view that exposure control with respect to letters of credit and guarantee facilities in a bank should be identical with that of funded credit risk?*

2. *Credit risk mitigants enable better credit mapping of exposures in a bank/financial institution. Explain.*

CHAPTER 10

Country Risk

1. Country Risk Defined
2. Direct/Indirect Country Risk
3. Composition of Country Risk
4. Country Risk exposure components
5. Modality of Country Risk Management
6. Important Macro Factors in Country Risk Assessment
7. Country Risk Exposure Provisioning
8. Contingency Plans and Exit Strategies
9. Questions

Risks surface not only within a country, but also in other countries where an organisation has business transactions. An Indian organisation may have outfits in a foreign country, and its transactions there falls within the ambit of 'country risk'. Obviously, there is no question of country risk as far as transactions within the home country are concerned.

COUNTRY RISK DEFINED

Michael Crouhy *et al* have defined country risk thus: "Country risk is the risk that a counter-party, or obligor, will not be able to pay its obligations because of cross-border restrictions on the convertibility or availability of a given currency" (*Risk Management*, page 297).

The Reserve Bank of India has defined this as: "Country risk is the possibility that a country will be unable to service or repay its debts to foreign lenders in a timely manner. In banking, this risk arises on account of cross-border lending and investment."

Kerily S. Brown in his book, *Investment Analysis and Portfolio Management* (page 120) offers a very simple definition of country risk. According to him, it is "uncertainty due to the possibility of major political or economic change in the country where an investment is located".

In short, country risk arises due to the risk of recovering exposures made outside the national borders of a country.

DIRECT/INDIRECT COUNTRY RISK

Direct country risk arises when an organisation has an operating centre abroad—i.e. outside its country of origin—and it has various financial commitments there. The probability of losses because of the commitments not being met when due is a potential risk factor. On the other hand, if an exposure is made within a country to a borrower having 'large economic dependence' in another country, the risk stemming from such an exposure may be treated as indirect country risk.

COMPOSITION OF COUNTRY RISK

The core of country risk is the risk of default in meeting financial commitments in the appropriate hard foreign currency like the US dollar. The following categories—singly or collectively—comprise country risk:

- Transfer risk: This occurs when there is a possibility of losses due to restrictions on external remittances of foreign currency. Though the obligor may be in a position to settle the debt in the local currency, he may not be allowed to convert it into acceptable foreign currency because of a foreign exchange crisis in the country.
- Sovereign risk: Although a sovereign nation is expected to be in a position to meet its liabilities at any point of time, there may be situations when countries fail to meet their commitments (loans availed of from other countries). Being sovereign entities, they cannot be subjected to the legal process (filing a suit).
- Non-sovereign/political risk: This includes the risk of losses

when the authorities in a country—armed with their sovereign power—take over the assets of a foreign entity and prevent it from discharging its liabilities. This may be caused by the political situation and the legislative power of the country concerned.

- Cross-border risk: This has two dimensions:
  i. Resident of one country having assets in another.
  ii. Exposure to local residents in the form of foreign currency.
- Currency risk: The value of foreign currency fluctuates against that of the country's domestic currency mainly due to economic/political reasons. When a commitment is undertaken in a foreign currency, the risk of an adverse movement may affect debt—both principal and interest—servicing.
- Macroeconomic risk: The risk of default may arise due to a severe macroeconomic crisis (for example, high interest rates on borrowing, low economic growth and the attendant scarcity of foreign exchange, weak legal system etc). This involves country risk when commitments are made outside the national borders.

COMPONENTS OF COUNTRY RISK EXPOSURE

Normally, exposures fall under two categories: funded and non-funded. In the context of country risk management, however, the RBI has different guidelines as far as banks are concerned. They include:

- Only funded exposure is to be considered.
- Applies only with respect to countries where a bank has a net exposure of 2% or more of its assets (gross exposure

minus tangible securities, acceptable bank guarantees and credit insurance).

- Funded exposures would cover the following assets:

i. Cash & bank balances.
ii. Deposit placements.
iii. Investments.
iv. Advances.
v. Trade credits/receivables.
vi. Overdraft in Vostro account.
vii. Remittances honoured under a drawing arrangement.
viii. Other monetary assets.

MODALITY OF COUNTRY RISK MANAGEMENT

The entire architecture of country risk management architecture revolves around the identification of risk countries and grading, measuring and monitoring of identified risk categories.

The Export Credit Guarantee Corporation of India Ltd (ECGC) has, based on its own expertise and experience, classified country risk into the following categories:

i. Insignificant.
ii. Low.
iii. Moderate.
iv. High.
v. Very high.
vi. Restricted.
vii. Off-credit.

As per RBI guidelines, banks operating in India may adopt the ECGC framework till such time as they frame their internal country risk rating systems. Banks should also **measure** the risk contents in an appropriate manner and insulate themselves against such risks by way of exposure provisions and build-up of additional capital. The RBI guideline also states: "Banks should use a variety of internal and external sources as a means to measure country risk. Banks should not rely solely on rating agencies or other external sources."

Country risk exposure should be controlled by setting up exposure limits. In this context RBI has *inter alia* laid down the following:

A) The country exposure limit is to be linked to the bank's regulatory capital (Tier I + Tier II) with a provision by way of a sub-limit for products, branches, maturity etc.
B) The exposure limit for any country is not to exceed the bank's regulatory capital except in the case of countries falling under the insignificant risk category (No. i above).
C) The regional exposure limits for country groups may be fixed if necessary.

The monitoring system should be comprehensive and ongoing, preferably on a real-time basis. In addition to the appropriate internal controls and concurrent audits when necessary, an assessment "of the impact of alternative outcomes to important underlying assumptions" may be made by way of stress testing of actual and potential risks.

IMPORTANT MACRO FACTORS IN COUNTRY RISK ASSESSMENT

1) Basics:
   - GNP per capita.
   - Credit growth.
   - Real interest rates.
   - Inflation rate.
   - Total exports.
   - Total imports.
   - Balance of payments.
   - Current account balance.
   - Foreign exchange reserves.
   - Total external debt.
   - Debt service ratio.
   - Unemployment rate.

2) Shockability: Whether pressured by excessive public sector spending and whether the budget is financed by IMF funding and current account deficits.
3) Politics: Whether there is political stability, and the form of government (democratic/non-democratic).
4) Internal economies: Whether appropriate measures to ensure fiscal austerity and control high interest burden if any are pursued.
5) External economies: Whether the currency was devalued recently (say two-three years before), and whether the current account position has improved because of the devaluation.
6) Whether any structural reforms were pursued in the recent past at the instance of the IMF/World Bank or at the initiative

of the country and what the position is at present.

7) Whether the economy and political system is healthy overall.

(Source: *Risk Management*, Michael Crouhy *et al*, page 310).

PROVISIONING FOR COUNTRY RISK EXPOSURE

The RBI has prescribed following scale of provisioning:

Sl. No:	Risk Category (as per the ECGC System) of the Country	Provision (% of Net Funded Exposure)
1.	Insignificant	0.25
2.	Low	0.25
3.	Moderate	5.00
4.	High	20.00
5.	Very high	25.00
6.	Restricted	100.00
7.	Off-credit	100.00

Notes

- The provision mentioned above will be over and above asset classification provision as per prevailing norms. However for 'loss' and 'doubtful' assets, both provisions taken together (country risk provision + asset classification provision) should not exceed 100% of the outstanding balance.
- No provision required for exposures to India.
- For exposures with a contractual maturity of less than 180 days, the country risk provision will be 25% of the above required provision (for example, 25% of 0.25% as in 1 & 2 OR 25% of 5% in 3 and so on).

- Banks may treat 'provisions for host country risk exposure' on a par with provisions held for standard assets (presently 0.25%) for the purposes of Tier II capital subject to the maximum of 1.25% of risk-weighted assets.
- In their annual accounts, banks must disclose the country risk position as under:
  - a) Risk category-wise country exposure.
  - b) Amount of aggregate provisions held.

CONTINGENCY PLANS AND EXIT STRATEGIES

It is obvious that any exposure beyond the notional frontiers of a country has a special dimension for the exposure taker. In these days of globalisation (and attempts to notionally eliminate, for the purposes of free flow of trade and commerce, the concept of national boundaries), organisations do endeavour to expand their overseas operations. Some public sector banks are reportedly going ahead with the expansion of branches/offices in various countries.

While there may be scope for expansion of exposures, especially in emerging economies, as far as existing country exposures are concerned, there should be an in-built mechanism to review on a regular basis the developments taking place in the macroeconomic, political and societal areas in various countries. These aspects have a strong influence on the risk grading of the country.

Organisations having country risk exposures should develop appropriate contingency plans and exit strategies. These are broadly on the following lines.

- Contingency plans should focus on all types of risk grades even though at a particular point of time there may not be any special problem attached to such an exposure. This is because in the event of an unexpected situation (for example, the September 2001 attacks in the USA), organisations should be in a position to quickly take steps to protect themselves from all types of business risks—credit, market and operational.
- Activation of contingency plans/exit strategies is normally resorted to at the eruption of any crisis.
- For country risk category No. 6 ('restricted' category) and 7 (off-credit category), a time-bound programme should be drawn (say two-five years) up to withdraw from such exposures. This can be done by crystallising the securities, transferring exposures, or by requesting parties concerned to repay exposures on mutually acceptable terms.
- Even in some rare cases where it is believed that waiting for an improvement may still perilous, some kind of financial sacrifice may be accepted in the exit process. From the cost-benefit angle in the long run, this may be useful.
- Contingency plans and exit strategies are complementary. A contingency plan may provide for an exit route. Similarly, an exit route strategy may be the outcome of a contingency plan activated in a crisis.

QUESTIONS

1. *Define 'country risk'. What factors would you consider while evaluating a country risk exposure?*

2. *Country risk provisioning is linked to the composition of country risk. Explain.*

3. *How would you devise contingency plans and exit strategies from the angle of country risk evaluation?*

CHAPTER **11**

Credit Audit

1. Credit Audit Defined
2. Objectives
3. Scope
4. Distinction between Credit Audit and Accounts Audit
5. Analysis of Components of Credit Audit
6. How Credit Audit is to be conducted
7. Model Formal of Credit Audit Report
8. Questions

Credit audit (also known as loan review mechanism) is the outcome of modern commerce, a result of the proliferation of credit/loan institutions the world over with sophisticated loan products on the one hand, and the growing concern about asset quality on the other. The core emphasis is on compliance with credit policy, procedures, documentation process and, above all, adherence to stipulated terms & conditions for sanction, disbursement and monitoring.

CREDIT AUDIT DEFINED

Credit audit is concerned with the verification of credit (loan) accounts, including the investment portfolio. Although the business of credit/loans is predominantly the domain of banks/financial institutions, any commercial institution can be involved in it as well—for example, credit sales creating accounts receivables.

Credit audit may be defined as the process of examining and verifying credit records from the viewpoint of compliance with laid-down policies, system procedures for the disbursement of credit and their monitoring. The RBI has defined credit audit as a mechanism to examine "compliance with extant sanction and post-sanction processes/procedures laid down by the bank from time to time."

Credit audit is not a statutory requirement. However, from the regulatory angle of credit risk management, the RBI has asked banks to implement an appropriate credit audit system for their loan/investment portfolios.

OBJECTIVES

Credit audit acts as an enabler in building up and monitoring asset quality without compromising on policies, norms and procedure. Its basic objective is implanted in the independent verification process, covering:

(i) The sanction process.
(ii) The modalities of disbursement.
(iii) Compliance with regulatory prescriptions besides adherence to existing in-house policies.
(iv) The monitoring mechanism and how it is suited to stop a possible decline in asset quality.

Thus an independent assessment (without being carried away by the judgment of those involved in sanctioning, disbursing and monitoring credit) is the 'whole and sole' of credit audit. The findings of the credit audit process, with the suggested course of action for improvements, operate as a safety valve for the organisation.

SCOPE

Credit audit must cover not only funded credit/loans—including accounts receivable—but also the investment portfolio, of both government and corporate securities. It should also cover non-funded commitments (letters of credit, guarantees, bid bonds etc). Individual account verification should be followed up by portfolio verification (for example, loan/credit portfolio on the whole, sectoral position, etc.)

The scope and coverage of such an audit depends on the size and complexity of operations of an organisation and past trends (say, over a period of three-five years) reflected in the individual/ portfolio quality of accounts.

DISTINCTION BETWEEN CREDIT AUDIT AND ACCOUNTS AUDIT

Although the basic element of both credit audit and accounts audit is verification/examination, the following points of distinction between the two are important:

Credit audit	Accounts audit
1. Concerned with loan/investment assets of an organisation like a bank/ financial institution.	1. Concerned with all types of assets and liabilities of an organisation.
2. This is not a statutory requirement even for a limited company (private/ public).	2. It is a statutory requirement (at least once a year) for all types of limited companies (no statutory requirement for others).
3. The scope of credit audit (otherwise known as loan review mechanism) is restricted to compliance with respect to sanction (loan/investment) and post-sanction processes/procedures as may exist in a bank.	3. The scope of accounts audit covers all assets/liabilities without any restrictions, but within the framework of the Accounting Standards of the Institute of Chartered Accountants.
4. Modality/periodicity may be decided by the financing institution subject to the regulatory guidelines of the RBI.	4. Modality of audit rests with the auditor concerned, who has to follow accepted financial practices/standards. For a limited company (public/private), an audit once a year is a must.

Credit audit	Accounts audit
5. The audit may be undertaken in-house by an organisation, and the auditor need not be a qualified chartered accountant.	5. Audit of limited companies (private/public) can be under-taken only by qualified chartered accountants.
6. Credit auditor is not required to visit borrower's factory / office, but frames his opinion only on the basis of records.	6. If need be, an auditor may not only verify the books of accounts, he may also physically inspect factory/place of storage of assets.

COMPONENTS OF CREDIT AUDIT

Sanction process: In a bank/financial institution, the sanction of a credit facility (funded loan as well as non-funded facility for example, guarantees, letters of credit, etc.) as well as investment in marketable securities have to go through channels fixed by the institution according to its needs and systems & procedures. Generally, the process goes through the following steps:

a) Receipt of credit application from the client at the operating unit, like the branch of the bank concerned.

b) Scrutiny of the application in the light of the bank's norms and guidelines as well as specific directives of the RBI.

c) Preparation of an assessment note (credit proposal) after verifying the necessary aspects of the borrowers and guarantors, if any (this includes credentials study, physical inspection of the business site/securities proposed as the case may be). For investment in securities, this involves details of the issuer, terms and conditions of securities, etc.

d) Exercise of the financial powers of the delegated authorities for sanction.

Disbursement modality: This is the consequence of the sanction process and includes:

a) Security documentation as per the terms & conditions of sanction.

b) Pre-disbursement physical inspection of the business site/ place for business lending.

c) In the case of acquisition of capital assets/investment in securities, direct payment to the seller/insurer concerned is to be made to ensure proper end-use.

Compliance: It is necessary that the bank/financial institution comply with regulatory guidelines and its internal norms/systems during the sanction process, the disbursement stage and the post-disbursement stage. In fact, throughout the tenure of any credit/ investment asset in the books, the bank/financial institution must ensure that no guidelines are breached. The RBI's new Risk-Based Supervision System will focus, *inter alia*, on the 'compliance' angle of the bank/financial Institution. Non-compliance may invite penal measures.

Monitoring: The credit audit process ensures that the bank/ financial institution concerned follows necessary monitoring measures so that the asset quality (loan/investment) remains at an acceptable level, and in cases of signs of deterioration, necessary rectification measures are initiated. Monitoring is an ongoing mechanism and in reality a safety valve for a bank/ financial institution.

Therefore, a credit audit is complementary to the entire credit risk management system.

HOW CREDIT AUDIT IS TO BE CONDUCTED

1. An in-house department may be set up with professionally qualified and experienced people.
2. In the alternative, an arrangement may be made with professional institutions to undertake such an audit (business process outsourcing).
3. Credit audit is to be restricted to the records mentioned with respect to appraisal, post-sanction supervision and follow-up.
4. Credit audit does not usually involve the physical verification of securities/visit to borrower's factory/premises.
5. The credit audit process may cover all credit records/ documents or a statistical sampling of a batch of records. According to RBI guidelines, in banks/financial institutions, all fresh credit decisions and renewal cases in the past three-six months (preceding the date of commencement of the credit audit) should be subjected to the credit audit process. A random selection of 5-10% may be made from the rest of the portfolio.
6. Credit audit is an ongoing process. However, for individual accounts, the frequency depends upon the quality of accounts. The audit may even be on a quarterly basis in the case of high-risk accounts, while it may be on an annual basis for low-risk accounts.
7. Large banks/financial institutions usually prefer to cover credit audit with a cut-off size (say, individual exposures of Rs 3-5 crore and over) on a half-yearly basis through their in-house officials.

RBI Guidelines on Credit Audit

Credit audit examines compliance with extant sanctions and post-sanction processes/procedures laid down by the bank from time to time and is concerned with the following aspects:-

Objectives of credit audit:

- Improvement in the quality of the credit portfolio.
- Reviewing the sanction process and compliance status of large loans.
- Feedback on regulatory compliance.
- Independent review of credit risk assessment.
- Picking up early warning signals and suggesting remedial measures.
- Recommending corrective action to improve credit quality, credit administration and credit skills of staff, etc.

Structure of the credit audit department:

The credit audit/loan review mechanism may be assigned to a specific department or the inspection and audit department.

Functions of the credit audit department:

- To process credit audit reports.
- To analyse credit audit findings and advise the departments/functionaries concerned.
- To follow up with the controlling authorities.
- To apprise the top management.
- To process the responses received and arrange for the closure of the relative credit audit reports.
- To maintain a database of advances subjected to credit audit.

Scope and coverage:

The focus of credit audit needs to be broadened from the account level to look at the overall portfolio and the credit process being followed. The important areas are:

- **Portfolio review:** Examining the quality of credit and investment (quasi-control) portfolio and suggesting measures for improvement, including the reduction of concentrations in certain sectors to levels indicated in the loan policy and prudential limits suggested by the RBI.

- **Loan review:** Review of the sanction process and status of post-sanction process/ procedures (not just restricted to large accounts). These include:
  - All proposals and proposals for renewal of limits (within three-six months from the date of sanction).
  - All existing accounts with sanction limits equal to or above a cut-off point, depending upon the size of activity.
  - Randomly selected (say 5-10%) proposals from the rest of the portfolio.
  - Accounts of sister concerns/group/associate concerns of the above accounts, even if the limit is less than the cut-off point.

- **Action points for review:**
  - Verifying compliance with the bank's policies and regulatory compliance with regard to sanction.
  - Examining the adequacy of documentation.
  - Conducting the credit risk assessment.
  - Examining the conduct of account and follow-up looked

at by line functionaries.

- Overseeing action taken by line functionaries on serious irregularities.
- Detecting early warning signals and suggesting remedial measures.

➢ **Frequency of review:**

The frequency of review varies depending on the magnitude of risk (say, three months for high-risk accounts, six months for average risk accounts, one year for low-risk accounts).

- Feedback on general regulatory compliance.
- Examining adequacy of policies, procedures and practices.
- Reviewing the credit risk assessment methodology.
- Examining the reporting system and exceptions to them.
- Recommending corrective action for credit administration and credit skills of staff.
- Forecasting likely happenings in the near future.

Procedure to be followed for credit audit:

➢ A credit audit is conducted on-site, i.e. at the branch which has appraised the advance and where the main operative credit limits are made available.

➢ Reports on the conduct of accounts of allocated limits are to be called from the corresponding branches.

➢ Credit auditors are not required to visit borrowers' factory/ office premises.

MODEL FORMAT OF CREDIT AUDIT REPORT

(RBI has not specifically prescribed any format)

Here's a model report for the credit audit for bank credit/loan accounts. The format may be modified to meet organisation-specific requirements.

GOOD BANK LTD.

CREDIT AUDIT

SPECIMEN REPORT FORMAT (ACCOUNT-WISE)

Period covered in the report (from .... to ....)
Credit audit report as on...

- Name of the borrower and group affiliation, if any:
- Main place of business/registered office:
- Date of establishment/ incorporation:
- Line of activity/business segment:
- Financing pattern:
  sole/multiple/consortium
  Share (percentage and amount of credit limit for such a lender):
- Date and authority of original sanction:
- Date and authority of last sanction/renewal:
- Credit rating by the bank/rating agency and what it indicates:

- Total exposure (funded & non-funded)
  To the party:
  To the group (if any):
  To state specifically if there is any foreign currency loan/commitment:

- Credit arrangement with the bank/financial institution: (Rs. in lakhs)

Facility	Limit/line	Outstanding	Amount of overdues, if any	Overdues since when

- Comments:

- Whether guidelines laid down have been adhered to while appraising/assessing:

- Comments on industry averages for inventory, receivables, creditors etc. taken into account:

- Comments on financial performance of the party vis-à-vis estimates and industry position, if available:

- Whether management quailties were analysed at sanction/renewal stage:

- Any other important issues:

- Whether all the terms and conditions of the sanction were complied with, if not details and reasons and when the same is expected to be done:

- Comments on first disbursements of facilities (applicable for fresh sanctions):
- Security cover stipulated as per sanction:
  Securities | Deficiencies, if any

- Security documentation:

- Date of document:

- Details of unrectified irregularities, if any:

- Whether charge filed with ROC (Registrar of Companies) for primary as well as collateral securities in case of a company, if not details with present status:

- Conduct of the account:

- Interest serviced up to (month/year):

- Submission of return/ statement by the party: Stock statement/statement of book-debts submitted up to (month/ year):

- Insurance for securities: Aggregate amount insured. Date up to which insurance policy will remain valid:

- Primary securities:

- Collateral securities:

- Physical inspection of securities:

- Whether pre-sanction inspection carried out and found in order.

- Whether post-disbursement inspection is regularly carried out and found in order:

- Date of last inspection:
- Accounts of group/sister/associate concerns

Name	Funded limit	Non-funded limit	Banking arrangement	Remarks of credit auditor on the account – if unsatisfactory, nature of deficiency.

- Suggestions of credit audit for remedial measures, where asset quality is showing signs of concern.
  a)
  b)
  c)
  d)

Date : Signature
Place:

QUESTIONS

1. *Define credit audit. Distinguish between credit audit and accounts audit.*

2. *Safe Bank Ltd. started operations recently. It has built up a loan portfolio of more than Rs 100 crore and has plans to expand the portfolio to Rs 500 crore over the next two years. Its present average loan asset size is between Rs 10 lakh and Rs 15 lakh but expects average size to go up to Rs 30 lakh.*
The bank has engaged you to advise on how it should instal a credit audit system and wants you to provide a model report format. How would you proceed?

CHAPTER 12

Risk Adjusted Return on Capital (RAROC), and Standardised and Internal Rating-based Approach

1. Raroc Defined
2. Objectives
3. Utility
4. Drawbacks
5. What is Standardised Approach
6. What is Internal Rating-based (IRB) Approach
7. Distinction between Standardised and IRB Approach
8. Probability of Default (PD)
9. Loss Given Default (LGD)
10. Exposure at Default (EAD)
11. Foundation IRB & Advanced IRB
12. Indian Situation
13. RBI Guidelines
14. Economic Capital Defined
15. Distinction between Regulatory Capital and Economic Capital
16. Computation of Economic Capital
17. Questions

The risk adjusted return on capital (RAROC) model, developed by Bankers Trust in the late 1990s, is rooted in the concept that the traditional way of evaluating returns from a loan (inclusive of investment) using interest and fee income does not provide a true picture of the credit risk efficiency of an organisation. This is so because it does not take into account the risk involved in various types of income-earning loan assets (including investment). In other words, unless the risk element of each loan asset (as also on a portfolio basis) is related to earning, effective pricing cannot be said to exist in the operation of any particular loan asset.

RAROC DEFINED

RAROC is a process/model concerned with adjusting net return (interest income + fee income – overheads) from a risk position with the estimated amount of unexpected losses arising from it and discounting it by its economic capital so as to activate an appropriate risk/reward environment across the organisation.

The RBI has defined RAROC as a system that "allocates a capital charge to a transaction or a line of business at an amount equal to the maximum expected loss (at a 99% confidence level) over one year on an after-tax basis."

OBJECTIVES

- To compute the appropriate capital charge (economic capital) on loans (including investment) after adjusting for the risk element.
- To facilitate the application of capital charge applying a hurdle rate (minimum acceptable return on a business activity).

- To provide a means of comparison with the benchmark return on assets (ROA) and RAROC derived after adjustment of risk premium.
- To estimate, as advised by RBI, the asset value that may prevail in a worst-case scenario and then to equate the capital to be provided for the potential loss.
- To provide for a mechanism to compare two businesses with different risk dimensions and volatility of returns and profiles and accordingly price loan (inclusive of investment) assets. Thus, a target pricing may be worked out.

UTILITY

- It acts as "the glue that binds a firm's risk management and business activities together" (*Risk Management*, Michael Crouhy *et al*, page 525).
- The economic capital necessary to protect an organisation from unexpected losses can be assigned appropriately, segregating, if necessary, by business type, product differentiation and customer classification.
- It provides effective, consistent and fact-based risk-adjusted performance parameters to enable the evaluation of business propositions from the risk-return angle.
- RAROC is the torch-bearer in the process of evaluation of an organisation's balance sheet on 'mark-to-market' basis.
- The RAROC mechanism can be forward-looking to enable the comparison of projected income over next one year on loans (inclusive of investment), or backward looking, facilitating comparison of actual income earned on loans (inclusive of investment) over the past one year. And in the process, computation of economic capital becomes easier.

Credit rating agency CRISIL has drawn up a practical example of the utility of RAROC method in loan pricing:

The RAROC Method of Pricing Loans		
Elements	**Example %**	**Source**
Funds transfer cost	5.45	Internal transfer pricing system
Required loan loss provision	1.25	Credit risk model
Direct expenses	0.70	
Indirect expenses	0.45	Customer/product accounting system
Overheads	0.40	
Total charge before capital charge	8.25	
Capital charge	2.76	Allocated equity/loan = 12% Opportunity cost of equity = 15%
Total required loan rate	11.01	After tax, capital charge is 0.12*0.15 = 1.8%
		Tax rate = 0.35
		Pre-tax capital charge = 1.80% / 0.65 = 2.76%

DRAWBACKS

- It is essentially a mathematical model, requiring a strong database, and can only be effective if the MIS of an organisation is reasonably compact.
- While measuring loan risk, there is often the practical problem of linking the charge in the market value of an asset (loan/ investment) with the duration of the loan and the extent of interest rate shown.

THE STANDARDISED APPROACH

This is a tool for measuring credit risk and, arising out of it, to facilitate specific regulatory capital requirements. For this purpose, the counter-parties in credit exposures (including investment) are classified into three categories:

i. Sovereign states.
ii. Banks (including development financial institutions).
iii. Corporates (besides limited liability parties, any others not falling under categories (i) and (ii), including exposure to partnership, sole proprietorship concerns).

This approach provides for preferential risk weights for each credit exposure (and also at the portfolio level) in the range of 0%, 20%, 50%, 100% and 150%, depending on the type of exposure and availability of credit risk mitigants (tangible securities, etc.). It may be stated that 150% risk weight is applicable to exposures classified as 'past due' unless specific provisions are already held.

INTERNAL RATING-BASED (IRB) APPROACH

This is also a tool to measure credit risk for regulatory capital (as of standardised approach), but its focus is more on the risk sensitivity of exposures and thus to provide discretion to use internal inputs for assigning preferential risk weights. The IRB approach acts as a support provider for disclosures to the market participants with information on asset quality of the specific exposure/group of exposures. IRB has two versions—the foundation version and the advanced version. In both versions, there are six exposure types:

i. Sovereign states.
ii. Banks (including development financial institutions).
iii. Corporates.
iv. Retail credits.

v. Project finance (loans for long-term projects, large in scale, of long duration and usually big risks).

vi. Equity (ownership interests in business concerns).

Any exposures not specifically falling in the above categories, including exposures to partnerships/sole proprietary concerns, are treated as corporate exposures.

DISTINCTION BETWEEN STANDARDISED AND IRB APPROACHES

While both approaches serve the basic purpose of measurement of credit risk and in the process, the computation of regulatory capital, the following points of distinctions are very important:

Standardised approach	Internal rating-based approach
1. It has three categories: sovereign, banks and corporates.	1. It has six categories: sovereign, banks, corporates, retail credit, project finance and equity.
2. It has no variants.	2. It has two variants: foundation and advanced.
3. It is simple and not sophisticated in terms of application.	3. It is sophisticated, requiring statistical tools.
4. It is not based entirely on the risk sensitivity of an exposure.	4. It focuses entirely on the risk sensitivity of exposures on the basis of estimates.
5. Regulatory risk weight prescriptions form the core of this approach.	5. Internal risk assessments supported by robust risk management process forms the core of this approach.

Standardised approach	Internal rating-based approach
6. No special capital incentive is provided from the prescription of regulatory capital requirements.	6. Appropriate capital incentives in terms of percentage reduction in risk weights (even to the extent of 90%) are available subject to the fulfillment of certain conditions. Lower regulatory capital of 2% to 3% may be possible.
7. Concepts like probability of default (PD), loss given default (LGD) and exposure at default (EAD) are not applied.	7. Probability of default (PD), loss given default (LGD) and exposure at default (EAD) are central measurable concepts in this approach.

PROBABILITY OF DEFAULT (PD)

It is a quantitative input that aims to measure the likelihood of the borrower defaulting over a specific time horizon. Its salient points are:

- PD should be computed with a database of a minimum period of five years.
- PD estimates may be possible through:
  - i. Internal default experience for the same category of exposures, for example, corporate exposures.
  - ii. Mapping made of data available from external sources in relation to the default situations.
  - iii. Statistical default models, depending upon the size and complexity of exposures.
- The percentage of PD is based on own estimates. Generally, a minimum PD of 0.3% is advocated.

LOSS GIVEN DEFAULT (LGD)

This input measures ***the proportion of the exposure that will be lost if a default occurs in an exposure***. Its salient features are:

- LGD provides the magnitude of a likely loss.
- This is expressed as a percentage of exposure.
- Exposures fully covered by trade receivables are accorded 50% LGD. Other securities may provide 40%.
- A database for seven years is useful in computing LGD.

EXPOSURE AT DEFAULT (EAD)

This is worked out at the time of default in an exposure. It measures the quantitative aspect of any facility (loan, OD, etc.) that is likely to be drawn and to which a bank/credit institution is already exposed to. Its salient features are:

- It is based on a bank's/credit institution's estimates.
- The database should be for a minimum period of five years.
- For a loan/OD, the amount already drawn and the amount not yet drawn but available under the line/limit are to be worked out. It may generally be assumed that the full amount was drawn at the time of default.

All the three quantitative inputs (PD, LGD, EAD) when combined provide a measure of expected loss. Example:

Expected loss = % of PD x % of LGD x amount of EAD.

XYZ Company Ltd. has an OD limit of Rs 1 crore with Mega Bank which has been fully drawn. PD for one year is estimated at 2% and LGD 50%. Expected loss will be:

(i) 2% of Rs 1 crore = Rs 2 lakh

(ii) 50% of (i) = Rs 1 lakh

FOUNDATION IRB & ADVANCED IRB

Overall, the IRB approach is more sophisticated and more risk-sensitive compared to the standardised approach. Within the IRB approach, a finer distinction is between foundation IRB and advanced IRB so that, over a period of time, the banking/financial system the world over can adopt the advanced approach in totality to more appropriately respond to the various risk elements in the business.

The major points of distinction are:

Foundation IRB	Advanced IRB
1. Values for loss given default (LGD) and exposure at default (EAD) are fixed and recommended to banks/financial institutions by the country's central regulatory authority (RBI in India).	1. Values for LGD and EAD are determined by each bank based on its internal default experience and default models in place over a time horizon of five-seven years.
2. Assessment of values of credit mitigants (collateral, guarantees) is done by the country's central regulatory authority.	2. Each bank/credit institution may assess the value of its credit mitigants.

Foundation IRB	Advanced IRB
3. For retail exposure, there is no foundation IRB (only advanced IRB where besides PD, the bank concerned will have to estimate LGD & EAD).	3. Advanced IRB is applicable to retail exposure also.

NOTE: PD for all types of exposures is to be estimated by the bank/ financial institution concerned in both the foundation and advanced approaches.

INDIAN SITUATION

The Advisory Group on Banking Supervision has indicated that it may take about five years for Indian banks/financial institutions before the entire system is fully able to meet the nuances of a sophisticated risk management system, including the adoption of the IRB approach. This length of time may be necessary because of:

- Lack of extensive computerisation and effective MIS management with reliable frequency historical data.
- Lack of qualified personnel.
- Lack of proper appreciation of sophisticated risk management concepts at the middle and senior management levels.

It appears from the Guidance Note of 12 October 2002 on credit risk issued by the RBI that banks in India are expected to move over at least to a foundation IRB approach to start with (from the existing standardised approach) for assigning preferential risk weights to their exposures.

To be eligible under the foundation IRB approach, the internal credit rating of the bank should comply with the following conditions:

i. Each borrower/exposure must have a ***rating***.
ii. In the credit rating system of the bank, there must be a ***minimum of eight grades*** of which a ***minimum of six*** must be for performing exposures and a ***minimum of two*** for non-performing exposures.
iii. The rating system should ensure that ***not more than 30%*** of the gross exposure of the bank falls in any one borrowers grade.
iv. Each individual credit rating should undergo independent review/approval by any other department (for example, loan review department).
v. Each borrower/exposure rating must be updated at least on an ***annual basis***.
vi. The bank board's approval is necessary for all material aspects of credit rating and PD estimates (LGD & EAD estimates will be provided by the RBI.).
vii. A mechanism should be created to obtain internal/external audit review of the bank's rating system together with quantification of ratings.
viii. Independent credit risk control units (for design, implementation and rating system performance) should be set up.
ix. Qualified and trained staff should deal with the rating process.
x. Under Pillar 2 requirements (Supervisory Review of Capital Adequacy), the bank's internal credit rating must be clearly linked with the bank's assessment of capital adequacy.
xi. A sound stress testing process must be in place.
xii. The internal credit ratings of the bank must have been in successful use for at least three years.

xiii. The bank must have a robust system to estimate PD.

xiv. Under Pillar 3 (market discipline), the bank must disclose its rating process, risk factors and validation system.

ECONOMIC CAPITAL—Concepts & Computation

In today's business world, 'capital' has undergone several phases of refinement. It is no longer restricted to owner's equity. From the risk management perspective, capital may comprise:

- Accounting capital (the amount brought in by the promoters at their discretion).
- Regulatory capital (the minimum percentage of risk-weighted assets as a cover for expected losses that is in place. Internationally, the minimum for banks is 8%. The RBI has, however, directed that they hold 9%).
- Economic capital (as a cover for unexpected losses to be determined by each bank).

Economic capital defined: Economic capital is the fund 'cushion' available in the business to absorb unexpected losses (that is, more than average or 'mean' losses) in credit portfolio up to a desired confidence level (expected losses are taken care of by regulatory capital). In allocating economic capital, the choice of confidence level (generally 99%) and risk horizon dependent upon the risk appetite of the organisation are very important.

The Risk Matrices Group has defined Economic Capital (*Risk Management Practical Guide*, 1999 edition, page 129) thus: "Economic capital is defined as an equity reserve or cushion for unexpected losses. It ensures that a company (bank) remains solvent and stays in business even under extreme conditions... Economic capital is comprehensive and covers all significant risks."

Distinction between regulatory capital and economic capital: As the RAROC model enables easy and correct computation of economic capital as distinguished from regulatory capital, it may be useful to distinguish these two from the risk management perspective:

Economic Capital	Regulatory Capital
1. Based on a mathematical model.	1. Rule/accord-based.
2. Aimed at absorbing 'unexpected' losses up to a certain level of confidence – ideally 99%.	2. Its purpose is to ensure that a bank/banking system has enough capital to take care of 'expected' losses.
3. There is no stipulated minimum (or maximum) level.	3. Only a minimum (internationally 8%, but as per RBI guidelines in India, it is 9% of risk weighted assets) is specified. It's up to the banks concerned to hold anything in excess of the stipulated minimum.
4. Reflects the risk content of business, thus protected with allocated capital.	4. May or may not signal the actual risk content in a business. The same level of capital is to be maintained both for top-rated and off-credit rated accounts.
5. Has a direct link to the pricing of the loan (investment) as unexpected losses are factored into the pricing.	5. Has hardly any role in pricing a loan (investment) asset.

Economic Capital	Regulatory Capital
6. The mark-to-market concept is the basis of economic capital. For this purpose, there has to be a liquid market for the sale/purchase of an asset or security.	6. The mark-to-market concept has no role to play in regulatory capital. Hence, the liquidity aspect is not considered.

Compution of economic capital: Since economic capital is allocated to cover unexpected losses as against expected losses, the steps for computing it are:

- **Step one:** Arriving at expected losses based on PD, LGD & EAD estimates of the credit portfolio.
- **Step two:** computing the standard deviation of expected losses.
- **Step three:** Fixing the desired level of confidence.
- **Final step:** Multiplying the amount of unexpected loss by a SIGMA number relating to the desired confidence level. The outcome will be economic capital.

Sigma – confidence level:

1.00 Sigma : 68% confidence level
1.65 Sigma : 95% confidence level
2.33 Sigma : 99% confidence level
3.00 Sigma : 100% confidence level

Generally, a confidence level of 99% (2.33 Sigma) as against 100% is considered, thereby allowing a probability of at least 1% that the actual loss may exceed the amount of economic capital computed as a protection from unexpected loss.

QUESTIONS

1. *Define RAROC. Give an example of the RAROC method of pricing loans in a bank.*

2. *What is the IRB approach? Do you think that the IRB approach is more focused than the standardised approach?*

3. *What are the prerequisites for adopting the foundation IRB approach in a bank?*

4. *Distinguish between economic capital and regulatory capital. Do you think economic capital provides an additional safeguard in the financial system?*

5. *Explain the concepts of probability of default, loss given default and exposure at default with examples.*

CHAPTER 13

Risk-Based Supervision

RISK-BASED SUPERVISION DEFINED

Risk-based supervision (RBS) is the monitoring and control of a business organisation—especially a bank/financial institution—by the regulatory authorities in accordance with its **risk profile**. All businesses have to take risks, and there is no place for a risk-averse organisation. But the risk appetite must be within the contours of the organisation's risk philosophy. This is precisely the reason why an external regulatory authority (RBI for the Indian banking system) periodically undertakes off-site as well as on-site examinations of the books/records of banks/financial institutions. The aim is to get first-hand information of their risk levels and, where necessary, initiate appropriate remedial/ preventive measures. Risk-based supervision operates as a regulatory tool to ensure the safety and security of the financial system. However, RBS is not a mandatory requirement under the Basel Committee guidelines.

RISK PROFILE DEFINED

The risk profile of a bank/financial institution is dictated by its size, complexity of operation, area of operation (especially when it has an overseas presence), its heritage and above all, corporate governance. Hence, its profile would vary from institution to institution.

The RBI has defined risk profile as: "The risk profile would be a document which would contain various kinds of financial and non-financial risks faced by a banking institution."

BUILDING BLOCKS OF A RISK PROFILE DOCUMENT

a) CAMELS/CALCS rating (details stated below) with analysis of the main features.

b) Volatility in the business segment.

c) Enforcement of a monitorable action plan (MAP) and assessment of the concerned bank's progress.

d) SWOT analysis of each business factor keeping in view the bank's size, capacity and area of operation.

e) Stress testing analysis of the bank's asset/liability and profit.

f) Analysis of lines of responsibility and accountability in the bank.

TOOLS FOR RISK PROFILING FOR BANKS

The entire portfolio is looked at from the angle of place of incorporation as under:

For domestic banks (banks incorporated in India) : CAMELS approach*

For foreign banks (banks incorporated outside India but having operations in India) : CALCS Approach**

* Evaluation under CAMELS approach:

- Capital adequacy (minimum to be 9% as per RBI guidelines)
- Asset quality (mainly for loan assets/investments)
- Management competence (corporate governance)
- Earnings (profits)
- Liquidity (cash + balance with RBI/other banks + marketable securities)
- Systems (procedures/practices of control aspects).

** Evaluation under CALCS approach:

- ➢ Capital adequacy
- ➢ Asset quality
- ➢ Liquidity
- ➢ Compliance***
- ➢ Systems.

*** This is an especially important parameter for a bank incorporated outside India to ensure that it complies with Indian regulatory prescriptions in addition to those home country regulations as may be relevant in its Indian operations.

Brief explanation of the above components:

Capital adequacy:	Minimum holding of capital (Tier I & Tier II) against risk-weighted assets. Under Basel norms, this should be a minimum of 8%. However, the RBI has prescribed a minimum of 9%.
Asset quality:	Computation of the build-up of loan/investment assets in the categories of standard assets, sub-standard assets, doubtful assets and loss assets. As per recent guidelines, another category called 'special mention assets' (which are **not** non-performing, but exhibit some danger signals) should also be taken into account in determining the overall asset quality of a bank.
Management competence:	Ability of the top management in running the institution smoothly and in compliance with regulatory norms and code of corporate governance.
Earnings:	Operating profit/loss position and build-up of the reserve fund.
Liquidity:	Level of cash + balances with the RBI/other banks and short-term readily saleable securities vis-à-vis holding of various categories of assets.
Systems:	Efficacy of operational practices/procedures and control environment.
Compliance (this is specifically applicable for foreign banks):	How effective is the compliance arrangement with regard to Indian regulatory requirements as also the concerned bank's home country guidelines.

OBJECTIVES OF RISK-BASED SUPERVISION (RBS)

- Articulation of explicit supervisory objectives and assessment of risk posed to such objectives and initiating remedial steps for the bank concerned.
- Off-site and on-site mechanism aligned to the risk profile of each bank.
- Continuous monitoring and evaluation of the risk profile of each bank keeping in view its business strategy and exposures.
- Development of a 'risk matrix' for each bank.
- Implementation of a forward-looking approach to rectify deficiencies, if any, quickly.
- Instituting a risk culture in the system through high-quality and reliable data, sound system and technology, effective risk control mechanism vis-à-vis the organisational set-up in the institution supervised.
- To initiate preventive measures to avert the contagion effect of a financial crisis in the banking system, like the Asian crisis of 1997.

FREQUENCY OF RBI'S RISK-BASED SUPERVISION

The supervisory cycle depends on the risk profile of a bank. Where, in the RBI's perception, the risk profile is significant, the supervisory cycle may be expected to be shorter—say, once in less than a year. And in low-risk cases, the supervisory cycle is expected to be longer—say, 15-18 months.

The supervisory cycle may operate as an incentive or a disincentive depending on a bank's position. Banks operating with low risk grading and a compact risk management system may have limited supervisory intervention as an incentive. While in other cases, sanctions and penalties may be imposed if the designed Monitorable Action Plan (MAP) fails. In such a situation, a specific prompt corrective action (PCA) may be enforced through an independent Supervisory Enforcement Cell of the RBI.

ROLE OF RISK-FOCUSED INTERNAL AUDIT OF BANKS

While risk-based supervision is the function of the Reserve Bank as the central banking authority in India, individual banks are expected to operate a clearly defined risk-focused internal audit system, which facilitates and smoothens the RBI's supervisory role. The internal audit department is to function independently as a control channel within the organisation.

Under the new RBS dispensation, the internal audit arrangement should place more emphasis ***on risk-focused audit rather than on mere transaction testing*** to verify the accuracy and reliability of accounts and records, testing of integrity, reliability and timeliness of the control report and compliance with legal and regulatory guidelines.

A risk-focused internal audit system is expected to achieve the following broad purposes:

- To provide checks and balances in a bank's risk management initiatives enterprise-wide as an ongoing function.
- To undertake the evaluation of adequacy and effectiveness of internal control systems.
- To examine the lines of control on risk process, effective-

ness of the corporate management function, especially with respect to safeguarding the assets and regulatory compliance aspects.

- Internal audit, besides suggesting remedial action on observed deficiencies, has a proactive role in protecting the bank from undue risk areas.
- Last but not the least, it aids the periodical risk-based supervision function of the RBI, since internal audit reports provide considerable insights into a bank's operations.

The RBI is reportedly having a re-look at the modalities of the proposed risk-based supervision before going ahead with this new supervisory tool.

QUESTIONS

1. *Define risk-based supervision. What are the building blocks of risk-based supervision.*

2. *A risk-based supervision system for a bank can be effective when it has in place a risk-focused internal audit system. Do you agree?*

CHAPTER 14

Credit Derivatives

'Derivative' refers to a substance/contract/instrument made from another underlying substance/contract/instrument, etc. Central Queensland University, Australia, in its *Publication on Advanced Finance* states: "The term derivative is used to identify a financial instrument that has been derived from another." A credit derivative is a stamped financial contract designed to reduce the possibility of losses arising from a credit transaction, facilitating the diversification of the portfolio.

According to Reily & Brown (*Investment Analysis & Portfolio Management*, 6th edition), a credit derivative is "an instrument whose market value ultimately depends upon or derives from the value of a more fundamental investment vehicle called underlying asset or security."

The Working Group on Credit Derivatives constituted by the RBI has defined a credit derivative as: "Credit derivatives are over-the-counter (privately negotiated) contracts. They are usually defined as off-balance sheet financial instruments that permit one party (beneficiary) to transfer credit of a reference asset which it owns to another (guarantor) without actually selling it."

Credit derivatives first appeared in the market in 1991 in the USA.

PRACTICAL EXAMPLE OF A CREDIT DERIVATIVE

Good Bank Ltd (GBL) has a large exposure to the diamond trade. It has decided, as part of its corporate exposure policy, to withdraw from diamond financing over a period of time—to start with, it wants to reduce credit risk to the extent of Rs 100 crore.

On the other hand, Flexible Bank Ltd (FBL) has a different perception of credit risk in the diamond trade. It is looking for credit risk exposure of around Rs 100 crore, but is unable to obtain the business directly, as all good diamond trading units are already banking with others.

Now GBL and FBL have different objectives:

- GBL wants to reduce credit risk by Rs 100 crore.
- FBL wants to take up credit risk for Rs 100 crore.

In this scenario, these two opposing objectives may be satisfied with a credit derivative in the following way:

- They enter into a financial contract.
- The terms of the contract would, *inter alia*, say that if GBL faces any losses in its diamond finance portfolio up to Rs 100 crore during the operative period, FBL would instantly make good the amount.
- In consideration of this risk being transferred to FBL (without, however, transferring the loan from the books), GBL would pay a premium (i.e., compensation for risk-taking) to FBL as may be agreed upon.
- The contract (i.e. credit derivative instrument) may be an over-the-counter trade item.

FEATURES OF CREDIT DERIVATIVES

- It is a financial contract involving, on the one hand, a ***credit protection buyer*** (CPB) and, on the other hand, a ***contract protection seller*** (CPS). Credit for this purpose means funded exposure by way of loans and advances as well as investment in securities.

- A CPB has to pay a fee—normally known as 'premium' in insurance parlance—to the CPS for undertaking the CPB's credit event risk. A credit event includes bankruptcy/ insurance, merger, default, crises default, repudiation, price decline, rating downgrade, etc. of the underlying asset for which the credit derivative agreement has been entered into.
- The settlement between the CPB and the CPS on the occurrence of any credit event may be on a cash basis or as agreed upon specifically between the parties.
- A credit derivative contract is structured as per the guidelines of the International Swaps & Derivatives Association.
- A credit derivative is an off-balance sheet financial instrument.

TYPES OF CREDIT DERIVATIVES

1. Transactions where credit protection is bought and sold:

   a) **Credit default swap (CDS):** Under this contract, the credit protection buyer pays a fee (premium) on a quarterly basis through the life of the contract.

   b) **Credit default option (CDO):** It is similar to CDS except that for the entire contractual period, fee is payable in advance.

   c) **Credit-linked note (CLN):** It is an on-balance sheet item (while normally credit derivatives are off-balance sheet items). The coupon or price of the note depends on the performance of the underlying asset against which the contract has been entered into.

d) **Credit-linked deposit/credit-linked certificate of deposit (CLD/CLCD):** It is structured as a deposit with default swap.

e) **Repackaged note (RN):** Issue of customised notes through a special-purpose vehicle.

f) **Collateralised debt obligations (CDOs):** These are made in connection with large credit exposures with collateral of underlying assets.

2. **Total return swap (TRS):** It is a contract aimed at replicating the economic returns of an underlying asset synthetically and covers both credit risk and market risk.

Although there are many varieties of credit derivatives as is evident from the above list, as far as the Indian market is concerned, it is proposed to begin with fairly simple credit derivative structures like credit default swaps, credit default options and credit-linked notes. Depending on the experience of the financial system over a period of time, the other types may be experimented with in future.

DISTINCTION BETWEEN CREDIT DERIVATIVES AND SECURITISATION

Both credit derivatives and securitisation involve transfer of credit risk of a loan/investment asset. However, there are several distinctions between the two:

Credit derivative	Securitisation
1. This instrument has no effect on the underlying asset of the credit protection buyer (CPB) as the relative asset continues to be in his books.	1. It involves the full transfer of the loan/ investment assets concerned from the books of the party for offering securitisation.
2. It does not involve the acquisition of any financial assets.	2. It involves the acquisition of financial assets.
3. It applies to performing assets only (non-performing assets excluded).	3. It applies to non-performing assets as well as performing assets.
4. It is an item of over-the-counter trade – unbundling credit risk from the credit instrument.	4. It is not an OTC trade item.
5. Sovereign risk can be hedged through credit derivatives.	5. The securitisation process does not generally involve sovereign risk.
6. Precondition for payment by credit protection seller (CPS) to CPB is the existence of any 'credit event'–bankruptcy, insolvency, default, etc.	6. No precondition, since the assets are fully transferred.
7. Documentation process is fairly standardised, involving nominal cost.	7. Transaction involves specific legal process and compliance, which often turns out to be quite expensive.

BENEFITS OF CREDIT DERIVATIVES

- **From the point of view of the credit protection buyer:**

1. Transfer of credit risk eases the capital adequacy requirement for banks/financial institutions.
2. Diversification of credit risk is possible, thereby building up a balanced portfolio.

3. Existing client relationships remain smooth even when the exposure limit is exceeded out of transfer of risk.
4. Depending upon the risk philosophy, risk policy and risk appetite, it is possible to manage credit risk portfolio without being affected by adequacy of funds.

- **From the point of view of the credit protection seller:**

1. Premiums provide a good source of revenue without any deployment of funds and day-to-day supervision.
2. Financial intermediaries—like insurance companies and mutual funds—are not in a position to take up direct lending exposure. Thus, credit derivatives enable them to be actively involved in the financial system for its orderly growth.

- **From the point of view of the operation of the financial system:**

1. Increased and efficient deployment of funds at the macro-economic level is possible, thereby fostering overall growth.
2. Pricing of exposures becomes more market-based as the initial risk taker has scope to transfer the risk.

DRAWBACKS OF CREDIT DERIVATIVES

- The economic size of a credit derivative internationally is a minimum of $10 million (Rs 46 crore approx.). It is difficult to obtain such a large underlying asset on a continuous basis in a developing country like India.

- The successful operation of a credit derivative depends upon the existence of a liquid secondary market, which is not present in many countries at the moment, including India.
- It is often difficult to assess the probability of a default correlation between the underlying asset and protection provider.
- Valuation of the underlying loan asset, which is not otherwise tradable, becomes difficult.

IMPORTANT PRECONDITIONS FOR ANY BANK UNDERTAKING AS CREDIT PROTECTION SELLER IN CREDIT DERIVATIVES

In the light of the report of the Working Group on Introduction of Credit Derivatives in India, the following preconditions are important:

- The activity must be closely supervised and controlled by senior management and the board of directors.
- There must be a clear separation between undertaking credit derivative transactions as a means of business development and monitoring, reporting and control-related issues.
- The bank must have a written credit derivatives policy, covering strategy, appetite and exposure limits.
- The discretionary powers of various functionaries to undertake the credit derivatives business have to be specified.
- There must be a clearly laid-down procedure for measuring, monitoring, reviewing and managing associated risks.
- There must be fair and cautious valuation of the risk management aspect of a portfolio.
- The credit risk envisaged must be in conformity with the

bank's normal credit approval and monitoring mechanism.

- There must be an appropriate system to deal with the likelihood of default correlation between the underlying asset and the protection provider.
- There must be an appropriate liquidity reserve procedure against uncertainty valuation of the underlying asset.
- An in-built system for pursuing the underlying borrower (like recovery procedure for loans & advances in a bank) when a credit event occurs must be created.
- Banks must use 'best market practices'.
- There must be a specific accounting & disclosure policy.

Above all, approval from the regulatory authority may be necessary for a bank that wants to take up the credit derivatives business for the first time.

DIFFERENCE BETWEEN CREDIT DERIVATIVES AND LETTERS OF CREDIT AND GUARANTEES

It is universally acknowledged that letters of credit (generally issued by banks) and guarantees (most commonly respected bank executed security) conveniently serve the objectives of 'transfer of credit risk' between two parties with ease and at low cost. What additional benefit can a credit derivative provide?

A credit derivative is an over-the-counter trade item, but L/Cs and guarantees obviously don't have this feature. As a result, the trade and commerce sectors find credit derivative products more acceptable, provided the regulatory and legal frameworks of a country are also business-friendly. Furthermore, credit derivatives provide a new business arena for some dominant players in the financial system such as mutual funds, pension funds/insurance companies, who are not permitted to issue L/Cs and generally also guarantees for third-party liabilities. Therefore, credit derivatives tend to reduce inefficiencies in the credit market and the gap left by the L/C and guarantee mechanism, and plays a different role in the financial system.

CAN CREDIT DERIVATIVES PLAY A ROLE IN THE UNIFICATION PROCESS OF THE INDIAN FINANCIAL SYSTEM?

Internationally, credit derivatives are playing an effective role in the process of unifying other active players in the financial system—like mutual funds, pension funds, hedge funds and insurance companies—imparting an element of efficiency in the credit market. Therefore, it is quite likely that the vast Indian credit market may embrace credit derivative products and align the same to the role of non-bank participants to ensure the more efficient utilisation of financial resources.

The underlying loan/investment market of credit derivatives may achieve an enhanced level of liquidity. Furthermore, the chances of the entire system facing an abrupt violent shock will be reduced since credit protection sellers will provide the necessary surveillance mechanism.

It is not possible to unify the entire financial system comprising bank and non-bank participants in all spheres of activities. Nevertheless, the fact that non-bank participants may operate mainly as credit protection sellers will surely act as potent drivers of the process of unification in the interests of the development of a more healthy and efficient credit market.

QUESTIONS

1. *Define credit derivative. Give an example of how it works.*

2. *Distinguish between credit derivative and securitisation.*

3. *What are the prerequisites to be fulfilled before a commercial bank enters the credit derivatives business?*

CHAPTER 15

Credit Risk in Non-Performing Advances

1. NPA Defined
2. Why NPA is a matter of concern
3. Why an Account becomes an NPA
4. Reasons for non-payment by borrowers
5. Lack of effective steps by Banks/Financial Institutions
6. Diversion of Funds—Who is to be blamed?
7. Action Flow Chart in NPA Recovery
8. Latest Legislation on Recovery of Advances
9. Staff Accountability
10. Main points in Staff Accountability studies on Credit Quality Slippage
11. Questions

Non-performing advances (NPAs)—known as non-performing loans (NPLs) in many countries—are generally the outcome of ineffective/faulty credit risk management by an institution. More often than not, the problem is not recognised at an early stage and hence remedial action is not initiated on time. This is precisely the reason why the RBI has advised banks (Credit Risk Guidance note issued on 12 October 2002): "Banks should have a consistent approach towards early problem recognition, the classification of problem exposures and remedial action."

NPA DEFINED

There was no statutory definition of NPAs in India till the promulgation of the Securitisation & Reconstruction of Financial Assets and Enforcement of Security Interest Act 2002. Now section 2(O) of the act defines an NPA as: "Non-performing asset means an asset or account of a borrower which has been classified by a bank or financial institution as sub-standard, doubtful or loss asset in accordance with the directions or guidelines relating to asset classification issued by the Reserve Bank." The RBI has directed that if in an exposure the payment of interest/repayment of instalment of principal or both remains unpaid for a period of 90 days (reduced from 180 days w.e.f. 1 April 2003), such an exposure is to be treated as being non-performing.

The basic criterion for an NPA is default—either on interest or principal instalment that is due—as per the terms of the contract. However, there is a subtle point of difference between an NPA and a defaulted account:

NPA	Default (in exposure)
1. Any interest payment and/or instalment towards the principal remaining unpaid for 90 days is considered an NPA.	1. Default occurs when it is determined that the borrower is unlikely to meet the obligation in full (no time horizon is specified).
2. NPA does not include the element of insolvency/ bankruptcy unless specific situations are observed.	2. Default may involve bankruptcy (inability to pay in cash irrespective of holding assets), insolvency (inability to pay even with the disposal of assets).
3. Globally, NPA is classified into three heads: ▪ Sub-standard. ▪ Doubtful. ▪ Loss.	3. No specific classification of default exists, although specific cases of wilful default are dealt with more severely.

WHY NPA IS A MATTER OF CONCERN

NPA management, especially in banks/credit institutions, is a very crucial function because of the following:

- Funds remain sunk without any returns in terms of cash flows.
- The credit cycle of banks/financial institutions gets choked up, causing liquidity constraints.
- Profitability is affected two-fold. One, on the provisioning for principal/interest charged. Two, nil income from the exposure.
- The capital adequacy ratio has to be maintained even when an exposure does not yield any return.
- Recycling of funds is affected.

WHY AN ACCOUNT BECOMES AN NPA

The Indian commercial banking sector has been passing through a phase of metamorphosis since the 1990's, when financial sector reforms began. Then, Asset Classification Norms and Income Recognition & Provisioning Guidelines were circulated, and the enforcement process was on. Along with this, there was an emphasis on credit growth, especially to the priority sector and small borrowers. As a result, there was both credit and NPA growth in the system. It is estimated that during the past decade, credit growth was around 90%, of which contaminated credit (NPA) accounted for a one-third share.

Broadly, two sets of factors are responsible for the increase in NPAs.

- Non-payment by borrowers due to various internal and external factors and, in some extreme cases, wilful default.
- Non-initiation of effective recovery steps by banks/financial institutions.

A. REASONS FOR NON-PAYMENT BY BORROWERS

According to the RBI (based on the speech by deputy governor Muniappan at the CII Banking Summit on 1 April 2002), the following are the main reasons for non-payment by borrowers:

Internal reasons:

a) Diversion of funds towards expansion, diversification, modification, new projects, and, in some cases, providing funds to associates/sister concerns with/without any interest.

b) Time/cost overruns of projects.
c) Business failure (product, marketing, etc.).
d) Strained labour relations.
e) Inappropriate technology/recurrent technical problems.
f) Product obsolescence, which again is a factor under (c) above.

External reasons:

a) Recession.
b) Non-payment by borrower's customers—both abroad and local.
c) Inputs/power shortage.
d) Price escalation (especially borrowers' products without the ability to pass on full quantum of increase to their buyers).
e) Accidents and natural calamities (massive earthquake in Gujarat recently).
f) Changes in government policies regarding excise duty/import duty/pollution control orders.

Wilful default:

So far, there has been no standardised definition of wilful default. The RBI guideline issued on 30 May 2002 only has the following 'examples' of cases of wilful default:

- Default occurs even when the unit has the capacity to honour its obligations.
- When the unit has not used the funds for the specific purposes and diverted them for other purposes.

- The unit has siphoned off the funds in breach of the specific purposes of the finance; the funds are not available with the unit in the form of other assets.

In essence, a wilful default may be defined as any non-payment of commitment by an obligor—even when there is no cash/asset crunch—with the sole intent of causing financial harm to a lender. A wilful default is generally the consequence of siphoning off funds by means of fraud/misappropriation.

Cases of wilful default need stern action, including filing of a criminal suit when so advised.

Quick mortality

Except in the case of wilful default, an account does not usually turn into an NPA in the short run. It may even take two-three years for these internal and external reasons to have a perceptible impact on the fulfillment of a borrower's financial obligations. In the interim, of course, a lender may get some warning signals. However, there are situations where the account shows symptoms of turning into an NPA soon after disbursement. Quick mortality of an exposure (account) occurs if signs/symptoms of full-scale default are noticed generally within a period of 12-18 months, forcing lenders to crystallise the securities and/or to initiate appropriate recovery steps.

The main reasons for quick mortality are:

- Siphoning off funds through fraud/misappropriation (wilful default) by the borrower.

- Sudden appearance of a cheaper close substitute product (this may, however, be considered as a factor of inefficient management).

Quick mortality is generally the outcome of wilful default.

B. LACK OF EFFECTIVE STEPS BY BANKS/ FINANCIAL INSTITUTIONS

Banks/financial institutions have to accept their share of the blame in NPAs by being ineffective in dealing with borrowers. The following main issues need to be mentioned:

- Inordinate delay in sanction and disbursement of need-based finance. As a result, borrowing units may be starved of requisite finance at the right time, forcing them to face financial losses. It is expected that banks/financial institutions should decide on a credit proposal generally within three-four months from the date of application.
- Lack of coordination between the financing institutions (especially in consortium/syndicated funding) and exchange of necessary information.
- Ineffective credit management, especially at the post-disbursement stage, and inability to detect and prevent unauthorised deployment/diversion of funds (like giving loans to associates/sister concerns).

  (RBI's Credit Risk Management Guidance Note of 12 October 2002 suggests *inter alia*: "Periodic visits to the plant and business site and at least quarterly management review of troubled exposures/weak credits. This is towards the improvement of credit management in banks/financial institutions).

- Timely recovery steps involving crystallisation of securities and/or legal actions not initiated.

DIVERSION OF FUNDS—WHO IS TO BE BLAMED?

Diverting funds availed for a particular purpose/project to unauthorised purposes/projects may turn an account into an NPA. The moot question here is: who is to be blamed for the situation? Is it that the borrower is solely responsible? Can negligence by banks/financial institutions be ruled out? It is difficult to come to any definitive conclusion. However, the following aspects need to be considered:

- Borrowers are expected to utilise the funds for the purposes for which they are availed. Thus, they are *prima facie* to be blamed/accountable for any diversion.
- Banks/financial institutions also have to exercise due diligence to ensure the proper end-use of funds. The credit risk architecture and management should be geared not only to detect any diversion at a later stage, but to prevent any attempt by borrowers to divert funds for unauthorised purposes. Post-disbursement supervision and follow-up should be effective. Merely obtaining appropriate covenants in security documents signed by the borrower may not be of use unless the appropriate system is in place.

ACTION FLOW CHART IN NPA RECOVERY

- To identify an NPA with the tool of credit rating (a considerable downgrade in a short period is a direct indication) and/or other tools (like depletion of security cover/

operation in accounts) and accounts that can be turned viable over time with a planned rehabilitation/nursing programme.

- Exiting unviable accounts by way of:
  i. Crystallisation/sale of assets.
  ii. Deciding on a compromise settlement with/without any sacrifice or to initiate legal action by filing a suit for the deficit, if any.
- Appropriate provisioning as per regulatory guidelines should be made/held for both viable and non-viable accounts during their subsistence. (In some countries, some provisions are made at the commencement of disbursement of any credit and are progressively increased as a 'buffer'. In India, as per RBI guidelines, even for accounts classified as standard assets, a minimum provision of 0.25% has to be made).
- Corporate debt restructuring (for accounts with an exposure of Rs 20 crore and above under consortium/syndicate/multiple banking arrangement) is to be initiated as per regulatory guidelines, considering that eligible accounts are viable.

LATEST LEGISLATION ON THE RECOVERY OF ADVANCES

Banks/financial institutions (holding security cover against an advance—except security cover by way of pledge/lien/shipping vessel/agricultural land) with an outstanding advance of over Rs 1 lakh with a further stipulation that the same should be over 20% of principal + interest, may enforce security interest by taking over the assets and sale thereof in conformity with the provisions under the Securitisation and Reconstruction of Financial Asset and Enforcement of Security Interest Act 2002.

STAFF ACCOUNTABILITY

Staff accountability means the process of exploring the reasons for any action/inaction on the part of a functionary relating to a particular subject/situation/matter. Accountability improves decision-making.

Professional management in an organisation demands professional decision-making, that is to say, for any action/inaction, there must be unambiguous and clear reasons—transparency being an essential ingredient.

In credit matters, decision-making by a functionary is multi-dimensional, beginning with the receipt of an application for credit and culminating in sanction or rejection. When sanctioned, the entire gamut of post-disbursement supervision and follow-up has to be carried out to ensure asset quality at any point of time. In the entire process, there may be cases when a functionary is negligent and/or dishonest in performing his role. Therefore, when a credit account (or for that matter in any decision-output) turns sour, staff accountability should be carried out with a three-fold purpose:

- Correcting/rectifying the officials responsible for the action/inaction and, in extreme circumstances, getting rid of such officials.
- Laying greater emphasis from the action point of view on *mala fide* acts as distinguished from *bona fide* acts.
- To reorient organisational rules/procedures/systems where necessary so as to be more focused on compliance.

In the Indian banking/financial system, staff accountability studies are generally initiated when the quality of an asset slips from the 'standard' category (also known as the 'pass' category in some countries), the main purposes being:

- Identifying officials responsible.
- Measuring damage in asset quality, linking it to lapses on the part of the identified officials.
- Taking appropriate actions (which may even include 'reskilling' the officials whose lapses were unintentional/ innocent ones) promptly against identified officials.
- The process may act as a deterrent for other officials, preventing any violation of norms/rules/guidelines.

MAIN POINTS IN STAFF ACCOUNTABILITY STUDIES ON CREDIT QUALITY SLIPPAGE

Staff accountability studies should be carried out on a 'watch-dog' basis and NOT on a 'blood-hound' basis. In order to ensure that such studies on credit failures are undertaken in a professional manner and free from bias, the following points should feature in such studies by a bank/financial institution:

- Finding out whether the credit proposal was appraised in accordance with the norms and guidelines laid down, including an investigation into the credentials of the proposed borrower/ guarantor.
- Checking whether the pre-sanction site visit/asset inspection was carried out and found in order.
- Whether the terms and conditions, securities and covenants

were stipulated as per the norms/guidelines laid down.

- Whether security documentation was in order and specific vetting of legal officials was done where necessary.
- Whether the first disbursement of credit was made after complete and perfect documentation and in compliance with all the stipulated terms and conditions of sanction.
- Whether post-disbursement supervision and follow-up was done as per norms and guidelines laid down.
- Whether all 'material' events noticed in any credit exposure were brought to the notice of the appropriate authorities, including communication to the Reserve Bank of India, if necessary.
- Whether any *mala fide* action/inaction on the part of any official was noticed.
- Views of the investigating officer as to the reasons for the slippage in the asset quality of an exposure.

In some banks, staff accountability is not examined for small loans up to Rs 25,000 unless a fraudulent act is suspected.

QUESTIONS

1. *Define NPA. Distinguish NPA and default.*

2. *What are the aspects to be borne in mind before a bank draws up an NPA recovery strategy?*

3. *The borrower is solely responsible in the cases of diversion of borrowed funds. Is it correct?*

4. *What is staff accountability? How would you look into the staff accountability aspects of a bank when its exposure turns into an NPA?*

CHAPTER 16

Miscellaneous Credit Risk

1. Is Zero Credit Risk a reality?
2. Ten similar-sounding but different concepts in Credit Risk Management
3. Questions

IS ZERO CREDIT RISK A REALITY?

Zero is a cypher, meaning no weight or implication of a matter, issue or situation. Zero credit risk in this context—viewed from a lender's perspective—suggests a credit exposure that remains intact without any diminution in its value in abstract terms at any point of time during its subsistence.

A very high quality credit appraisal, post-disbursement supervision and follow-up may, in most situations, facilitate the maintenance of asset quality of exposures at the individual and portfolio levels without any downgrade. But expecting a credit exposure to have zero risk at all times is a Utopian dream.

Statistical analysis does not support 100% certainty in recovering exposures in any situation whatsoever. Some element of risk will always remain, even in a latent form, whatever the quality of appraisal and supervision for an exposure. Even if we take the case of loans against time deposits by a bank, the 'spread risk' —i.e. the difference between the rate of interest chargeable on a loan and payable on the deposit—remains. This may not be protected if the margin against the value of the deposit is not substantial (usually, banks in India stipulate a 5% margin, and in some extreme cases, no margin whatsoever).

Thus, the risk in a credit exposure does not vanish, forcing the lenders to decide from time to time which exposure to retain and which to shed.

Thus, zero risk is a myth, and not a reality.

TEN SIMILAR-SOUNDING BUT DIFFERENT CONCEPTS IN CREDIT RISK MANAGEMENT

1. **Credit philosophy and credit policy:** The credit philosophy of a bank/financial institution is concerned with maintaining a healthy and high-quality credit portfolio in consonance with regulatory prescriptions and the risk management framework. Credit policy, on the other hand, embraces prioritising extension of credit with a timely credit delivery system taking into account pricing and quality of exposure.

2. **Credit delivery and credit deployment:** Credit delivery involves providing need-based credit facilities to various productive and social sectors for approved purposes speedily and at low cost. Credit deployment ensures that liquidity management is undertaken in such a manner that, while adhering to credit philosophy and credit policy, the bank/financial institution deploys funds so as to earn the maximum returns.

3. **Credit delivery/loan delivery:** While credit delivery connotes a package of credits as mentioned above, loan delivery is a specific regulatory guideline (of the RBI) under which banks that provide working capital to large borrowers beyond a cut-off point (Rs 10 crore) have to segregate the cash credit component (running facility) and loan component (to be repayable over a specified time frame).

4. **Credit tier/capital tier:** Credit tier essentially includes the various functional levels in banks/financial institutions through which a credit application passes through for eventual sanc-

tion or rejection (however, priority sector proposals in some cases are not rejected at lower levels). Capital tier refers to the minimum fund base (Tier I & Tier II) against risk-weighted assets that banks/financial institutions need to maintain. Internationally, this is a minimum of 8%. (The RBI has, however, prescribed a minimum of 9%).

5. **Credit negative/credit discretionary:** No advance can be granted for any illegal/immoral purposes or that which is opposed to public policy, like smuggling, speculation, etc. This may be treated as a credit negative. Credit discretionary covers all credit applications that are processed/considered according to the lender's discretion keeping in view that no applicant can demand credit as a matter of right.

6. **Credit migration/credit mitigation:** Credit migration refers to the movement of a credit exposure from one rating grade to another rating grade (in a credit rating system) so as to reflect asset quality at any particular point of time. Migration may be both upward (from AA to AAA, etc.) or downward (from AA to A). Credit mitigation means reduction of credit risk in an exposure by a safety net of tangible and realisable securities, including third-party approved guarantees/insurance.

7. **Take-over credit/take-out credit:** Take-over credit is when a borrower switches its credit account from one bank/financial institution to another. This usually arises both for the advantage of the borrower (reduction of rate of interest, etc.) and the lender (deployment of funds). Take-out credit occurs when a lender, after maintaining a large credit expo-

sure, passes it on to another lender at a later stage. This is close to asset-sale for recycling of funds.

8. **Credit margin/credit haircut:** Credit margin is the specific percentage reduction in the declared value of securities for computing the drawing power against them on an ongoing basis. It is security-specific (say, margin on raw materials is 25%, etc.). Credit haircut also involves the specific percentage reduction in the value of the securities, taking into account the risk-weight of the exposure as may be reflected in its credit rating. Thus, besides being security-specific, haircut takes into account the risk weight of a particular credit account.

9. **Prime rate/hurdle rate:** Prime rate is the rate of interest on a credit facility for the top-rated borrowers of a bank/financial institution. Such a rate is generally lower than for other credit accounts. Hurdle rate is the minimum acceptable rate of return on a business activity.

10. **Absolute write-off/prudential write-off:** When an outstanding balance in a credit account is charged off from bank/financial institution's account books (without sacrificing its right to recovery), it is treated as an absolute write-off. In some circumstances, however, the outstanding balance is transferred by the operating unit (branch) to its head office and is thus removed from the book of accounts of the branch concerned. This is known as prudential write-off.

QUESTIONS

1. *Credit risk in an exposure can never be reduced to zero. Explain with an example.*

2. *Do you think that from Credit Risk Management angle there can be any Credit Policy without a Credit Philosophy of an organisation though with appropriate credit delivery and credit mitigation measures?*

GLOSSARY

Backtesting: The specific process of testing the validity of a proposition/model in the light of the forecasts or assumed results.

Basel Committee: An international committee operating from Basel (Switzerland) in charge of ensuring global banking/risk regulations.

Basis Risk: The likely loss arising out of the change in interest rate/pricing difference of a class of assets/liabilities.

Benchmarking: Comparison of an aspect/parameter (e.g. current ratio, percentage of net profit on sales) with the best in the industry/sector.

Credit Derivative: Instrument of reduction of risk and diversification of an underlying credit portfolio.

Credit Risk: The possibility of loss due to a decline in the quality of a loan asset.

Credit Policy: General outline of extension of credit facilities with acceptable risk parameters and on debt collection.

Credit Risk Model: Quantitative study of credit risk covering both 'good' and 'bad' borrowers.

Credit Paradox: Situations where credit propositions with a higher spread have higher risk and those with lower spread have lower risk, and the lender is perplexed as to what he should do.

***Credit Risk Mitigation*:** Reduction in credit risk through marketable collateral securities, credit derivatives/guarantees.

***Country Risk*:** Risk of the eventual recovery of a credit exposure undertaken outside the national borders of a country.

***Credit Rationing*:** Restrictions on the amount of loan to a borrower/borrower class with higher rate of interest beyond a cut-off amount/quantitative restrictions.

***Credit Audit*:** Process of examination and verification of credit records from the viewpoint of compliance with policies, systems, procedures.

***Credit Value at Risk (Credit VAR)*:** Estimate of the potential loss in a single credit/credit portfolio over a period, usually of one year, based on a level of certainty.

***Credit Mortality Rate*:** Historic default rate of credit exposure.

***Corporate Exposure*:** Exposure to companies, partnerships, proprietorships or any other incorporated/registered organization (thus, 'corporate' does not imply only public/private limited companies).

***Confidence Level*:** A statistical prediction of a level of certainty.

***Credit Concentration*:** Risk concentration in any single/group exposure with the potential of large losses affecting the organisation's well-being and core operations.

***Credit Quality*:** The relative likelihood of default in a credit account over a given period.

GLOSSARY

***Credit Portfolio*:** A collection of various credit accounts.

***Duration*:** The process of arriving at the weighted average term of cash flow from a financial instrument.

***Distance of Default*:** A level of asset value between total liabilities and short-term debt.

***Economic Capital*:** Owned fund set aside to absorb unexpected losses.

***Exposure at Default (EAD)*:** Quantitative aspect of any facility (in default) that is likely to be drawn as per already agreed terms.

***Fat Tails*:** Larger number of occurrences of any event (e.g. defaults) away from the mean than estimated by standard deviation.

***Fourth Market*:** Direct trading of securities/assets without the assistance of any brokers.

***Greek Measure*:** Set of specialized risk measures in respect of the sensitivities of derivative instruments.

***Hair Cut*:** Reduction in the value of collateral by a specific value/percentage.

***Investment*:** Deployment of savings (resources) to increase their value in the future.

***Loss Given Default (LGD)*:** Likelihood of the loss of the proportion of the exposure if default occurs.

***Model Risk*:** Risk arising out of the use of mathematical models for valuation/mitigation of securities.

***Market Risk*:** Risk of a possible loss due to changes in market variables.

***Non-performing Asset (NPA)*:** Asset/account whose interest/ instalment remains unpaid for a period of 90 days.

***Operational Risk*:** Risk of a possible loss due to failure of systems, procedures, people or external events.

***Probability of Default (PD)*:** Quantitative input of the likelihood of default over a specific time horizon.

***Quick Mortality*:** Occurrence of signs/systems of full-scale default of an exposure within 12-18 months.

***Risk*:** Probability of loss due to an unexpected event.

***Risk Mapping*:** Process of estimating current and future magnitudes of risk elements.

***Risk Appetite*:** Objective of maximizing earnings within the contours of risk perception.

***Risk Philosophy*:** Objective of developing and maintaining a healthy portfolio within the legal/regulatory framework.

***RAROC*:** Model facilitating the allocation of capital charge to a transaction/business on the basis of maximum expected losses over one year.

Settlement Risk: Risk of a possible failure in the completion/ settlement of a financial transaction.

Stress Testing: In the worst-case situation, the value of asset may fall. The technique used for arriving at such a position is stress testing.

Small & Medium Enterprise (SME): As per the Basel Committee, borrowers with annual sales of less than 50 million euros (Rs.225 crore approx.) are to be treated as SMEs.

Subordinated Credit: Unsecured credit where the borrower's assets are used to secure other creditors.

Three Pillars: Basel Committee principle on (i) Capital adequacy, (ii) Supervisory process (iii) market discipline.

Value at Risk (VAR): A measure of the probability of losses for a given time period of holding an exposure.

Zero Risk: Probability of an exposure remaining intact without any diminution in its value during its subsistence.

RBI GUIDANCE NOTE DATED 12.10.2002

Policy Framework

1.1 Credit risk is defined as ***the possibility of losses associated with diminution in the credit quality of borrowers or counterparties. In a bank's portfolio, losses stem from outright default due to inability or unwillingness of a customer or counter-party to meet commitments in relation to lending, trading, settlement and other financial transactions. Alternatively, losses result from reduction in portfolio value arising from actual or perceived deterioration in credit quality***. Credit risk emanates from a bank's dealings with an individual, corporate, bank, financial institution or a sovereign. Credit risk may take the following forms:

⇒ *in the case of direct lending: principal/and or interest amount may not be repaid;*

⇒ *in the case of guarantees or letters of credit: Funds may not be forthcoming from the constituents upon crystallization of the liability;*

⇒ *in the case of treasury operations: The payment or series of payments due from the counter parties under the respective contracts may not be forth-coming or ceases;*

⇒ *in the case of securities trading businesses: funds/*

securities settlement may not be effected;

⇒ *in the case of cross-border exposure: the availability and free transfer of foreign currency funds may either cease or restrictions may be imposed by the sovereign.*

1.2 In this backdrop, it is imperative that banks have a robust credit risk management system which is sensitive and responsive to these factors. The effective management of credit risk is a critical component of comprehensive risk management and is essential for the long term success of any banking organisation. Credit risk management encompasses identification, measurement, monitoring and control of the credit risk exposures.

1.3 Building Blocks of Credit Risk Management

In a bank, an effective credit risk management framework would comprise of the following distinct building blocks:

a) Policy and Strategy

b) Organisational Structure

c) Operations/Systems

1.4 Policy and Strategy

The Board of Directors of each bank shall be responsible for approving and periodically reviewing the credit risk strategy and significant credit risk policies.

1.4.1 Credit Risk Policy

❖ Every bank should have a credit risk policy document

approved by the Board. The document should include risk identification, risk measurement, risk grading/aggregation techniques, reporting and risk control/mitigation techniques, documentation, legal issues and management of problem loans.

- Credit risk policies should also define target markets, risk acceptance criteria, credit approval authority, credit origination/maintenance procedures and guidelines for portfolio management.
- The credit risk policies approved by the Board should be communicated to branches/controlling offices. All dealing officials should clearly understand the bank's approach for credit sanction and should be held accountable for complying with established policies and procedures.
- Senior management of a bank shall be responsible for implementing the credit risk policy approved by the Board.

1.4.2 Credit Risk Strategy

- Each bank should develop, with the approval of its Board, its own credit risk strategy or plan that establishes the objectives guiding the bank's credit-granting activities and adopt necessary policies/procedures for conducting such activities. This strategy should spell out clearly the organisation's credit appetite and the acceptable level of risk-reward trade-off for its activities.

- The strategy would, therefore, include a statement of the bank's willingness to grant loans based on the type of economic activity, geographical location, currency, market, maturity and anticipated profitability. This would necessarily translate into the identification of target markets and business sectors, preferred levels of diversification and concentration, the cost of capital in granting credit and the cost of bad debts.
- The credit risk strategy should provide continuity in approach and also take into account the cyclical aspects of the economy and the resulting shifts in the composition/quality of the overall credit portfolio. This strategy should be viable in the long run and through various credit cycles.
- Senior management of a bank shall be responsible for implementing the credit risk strategy approved by the Board.

1.5 Organisational Structure

Sound organisational structure is *sine qua non* for the successful implementation of an effective credit risk management system. The organisational structure for credit risk management should have the following basic features:

*The **Board of Directors** should have the overall responsibility for management of risks. The Board should decide the risk management policy of the bank and set limits for liquidity, interest rate, foreign exchange* *and equity price risks.*

*The **Risk Management Committee** will be a Board level sub committee including the CEO and heads of Credit, Market and Operational Risk Management Committees. It will devise the policy and strategy for integrated risk management containing various risk exposures of the bank including credit risk. For this purpose, this committee should effectively coordinate between the Credit Risk Management committee (CRMC), the Asset Liability Management committee and other risk committees of the bank, if any. It is imperative that the independence of this committee is preserved. The Board should, therefore, ensure that this is not compromised at any cost. In the event of the Board not accepting any recommendation of this committee, systems should be put in place to spell out the rationale for such an action and should be properly documented. This document should be made available to the internal and external auditors for their scrutiny and comments. The credit risk strategy and policies adopted by the committee should be effectively communicated throughout the organisation.*

1.5.1 Each bank may, depending on the size of the organisation or loan/investment book, constitute a high-level **Credit Risk Management Committee (CRMC)**. The committee should be headed by the chairman/CEO/ED, and should comprise the heads of Credit Department, Treasury, Credit Risk Management Department (CRMD) and the Chief Economist. The functions of the Credit

TYPICAL ORGANISATIONAL STRUCTURE FOR RISK MANAGEMENT

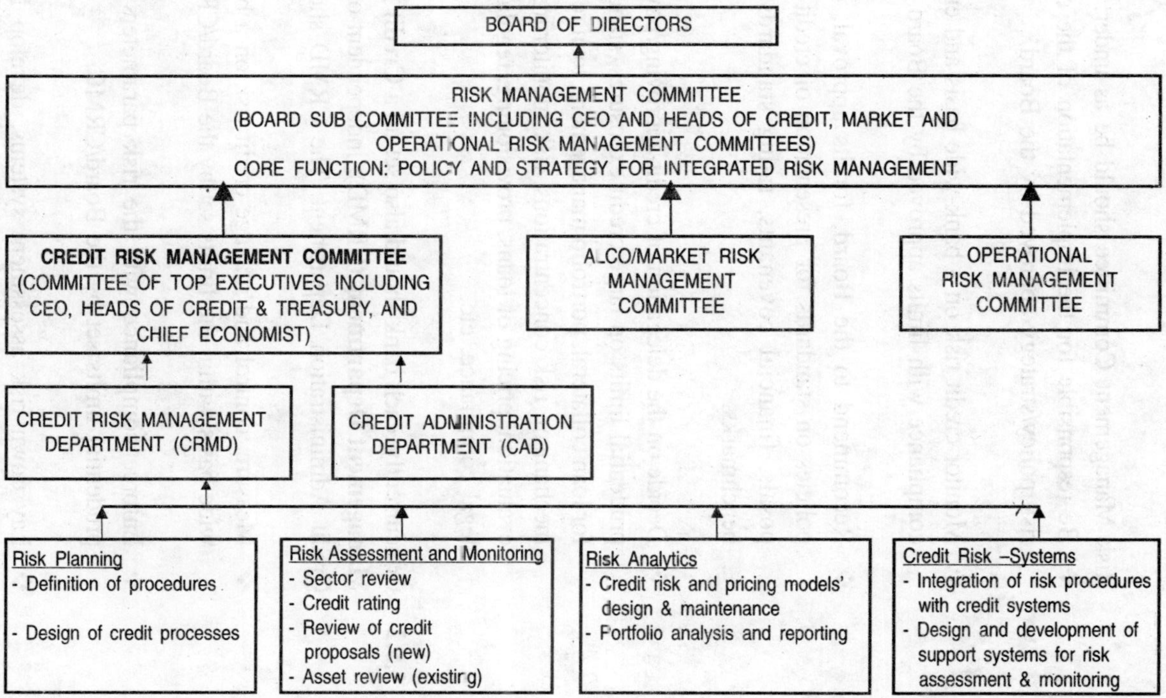

Risk Management Committee should be as under:

- Be responsible for the implementation of the credit risk policy/strategy approved by the Board.

- Monitor credit risk on a bank-wide basis and ensure compliance with limits approved by the Board.

- Recommend to the Board, for its approval, clear policies on standards for presentation of credit proposals, financial covenants, rating standards and benchmarks.

- Decide on the delegation of credit-approving powers, prudential limits on large credit exposures, standards for loan collateral, portfolio management, loan review mechanism, risk concentrations, risk monitoring and evaluation, pricing of loans, provisioning, regulatory/ legal compliance, etc.

1.5.2 Concurrently, each bank should also set up a **Credit Risk Management Department** (CRMD), independent of the Credit Administration Department. The CRMD should:

- Measure, control and manage credit risk on a bank-wide basis within the limits set by the Board/CRMC

- Enforce compliance with the risk parameters and prudential limits set by the Board/CRMC.

- Lay down risk assessment systems, develop MIS, monitor the quality of the loan/investment portfolio, identify problems, correct deficiencies and undertake loan review/audit. Large banks could consider a separate set-up for loan review/audit.

- Be accountable for protecting the quality of the entire loan/investment portfolio. The Department should undertake portfolio evaluations and conduct comprehensive studies on the environment to test the resilience of the loan portfolio.

1.6 Operations/Systems

Banks should have in place appropriate credit administration, credit risk measurement and monitoring processes. The credit administration process typically involves the following phases:

- *Relationship management phase,* i.e., business development.

- *Transaction management phase,* covers risk assessment, loan pricing, structuring the facilities, internal approvals, documentation, loan administration, ongoing monitoring and risk measurement.

- *Portfolio management phase,* entails monitoring of the portfolio at a macro level and the management of problem loans.

On the basis of the broad management framework stated above, the banks should have the following credit risk measurement and monitoring procedures:

- Banks should establish proactive credit risk management practices like annual/half yearly industry studies and individual obligor reviews, periodic credit calls that are documented, periodic visits of plant and business site, and at least quarterly management reviews of troubled exposures/weak credits.

- Banks should have a system of checks and balances in place for extension of credit viz:
  - Separation of credit risk management from credit sanction
  - Multiple credit approvers, making financial sanction subject to approvals at various stages—viz credit ratings, risk approvals, credit approval grid, etc.
  - An independent audit and risk review function.

- The level of authority required to approve credit will increase as amounts and transaction risks increase and as risk ratings worsen.

- Every obligor and facility must be assigned a risk rating.

- Mechanism to price facilities depending on the risk grading of the customer, and to attribute accurately the associated risk weightings to the facilities.

- Banks should ensure that there are consistent standards for the origination, documentation and maintenance for extensions of credit.

- Banks should have a consistent approach towards early problem recognition, the classification of problem exposures, and remedial action.

- Banks should maintain a diversified portfolio of risk assets, have a system to conduct regular analysis of the portfolio and to ensure on-going control of risk concentrations.

- Credit risk limits include obligor limits and concentration limits by industry or geography. The Boards should authorise efficient and effective credit approval processes for operating within the approval limits.

- In order to ensure transparency of risks taken, it is the responsibility of banks to accurately, completely, and in a timely fashion, report the comprehensive set of credit risk data to the independent risk system.

- Banks should have systems and procedures for monitoring the financial performance of customers and for keeping outstanding within limits.

- A conservative policy for provisioning in respect of non-performing advances may be adopted.

- Successful credit management requires experience, judgement and commitment to technical development. Banks should have a clear, well-documented scheme of delegation of powers for credit sanction.

Banks must have a Management Information System (MIS), which should enable them to manage and measure the credit risk inherent in all on- and off-balance sheet activities. The MIS should provide adequate information on the composition of the credit portfolio, including identification of any concentration of risk. Banks should price their loans according to the risk profile of the borrower and the risks associated with the loans.

Credit Rating Framework

2.1 Background

A Credit-risk Rating Framework (CRF) is necessary to avoid the limitations associated with a simplistic and broad classification of loans/exposures into a "good" or a "bad" category. The CRF deploys a number/alphabet/symbol as a primary summary indicator of risks associated with a credit exposure. Such a rating framework is the basic module for developing a credit risk management system and all advanced models/approaches are based on this structure. In spite of the advances in risk management techniques, CRF continues to be used to a great extent. These frameworks have been primarily driven by a need to standardise and uniformly communicate the "judgement" in credit selection procedures and are not a substitute to the vast lending experience accumulated by the banks' professional staff.

2.2 End Use of Risk-Ratings made on the CRF

Broadly, CRF can be used for the following purposes:

a. Individual credit selection, wherein either a borrower or a particular exposure/facility is rated on the CRF.

b. Pricing (credit spread) and specific features of the loan facility. This would largely constitute transaction-level analysis.

c. Portfolio-level analysis.

d. Surveillance, monitoring and internal MIS.

e. Assessing the aggregate risk profile of bank/lender. These would be relevant for portfolio-level analysis. For instance, the spread of credit exposures across various CRF categories, the mean and the standard deviation of losses occurring in each CRF category and the overall migration of exposures would highlight the aggregated credit-risk for the entire portfolio of the bank.

2.3 Basic Architecture of CRFs

The following elements outline the basic architecture and the operating principles of any CRF.

2.3.1 Grading system for calibration of credit risk

- Nature of grading system
- Number of grades used
- Key outputs of CRF

2.3.2 Operating design of CRF

- Which exposures are rated?
- The risk rating process
- Assigning and monitoring risk ratings
- The mechanism of arriving at risk ratings
- Standardisation and benchmark for risk ratings
- Written communications and formality of procedures

2.3.3 CRFs and Portfolio Credit Risk

- Portfolio surveillance and reporting
- Adequate levels of provisioning for credit events

- Guidelines for asset build-up, aggregate profitability and pricing
- Interaction with external credit assessment institutions

The architecture and operating principles are discussed in detail in the ensuing paragraphs.

2.4 Grading System for Calibration of Credit Risk

The grades (symbols, numbers, alphabets, descriptive terms) used in the internal credit-risk grading system should represent, without any ambiguity, the default risks associated with an exposure. The grading system should enable comparisons of risks for purposes of analysis and top management decision-making. It should also reflect regulatory requirements of the supervisor on asset classification (e.g. the RBI asset classification). It is anticipated that, over a period of time, the process of risk identification and risk assessment will be refined further. The grading system should, therefore, be flexible and should accommodate the refinements in risk categorisation.

2.4.1 Nature of Grading System for the CRF

The grading system adopted in a CRF could be an alphabetic or numeric or an alpha-numeric scale. Since rating agencies follow a particular scale (AAA, AA+, BBB etc.), it would be prudent to adopt a different rating scale to avoid confusion in internal communications. Besides, adoption of a different rating scale would permit comparable benchmarking between the two mechanisms. Several banks utilise a numeric rating scale. The number of grades for the "acceptable" and the "unacceptable" credit risk categories would depend on the finesse of risk gradation. Normally, numeric scales developed for CRFs are such that the lower the credit-risk, the lower is the calibration on the scale.

> ***Illustration***
>
> A rating scale could consist of 9 levels, of which levels 1 to 5 represent various grades of acceptable credit risk and levels 6 to 9 represent various grades of unacceptable credit risk associated with an exposure.
>
> The scale, starting from "1" (which would represent the lowest level of credit risk and the highest level of safety/ comfort) and ending at "9" (which would represent the highest level of credit risk and the lowest level of safety/ comfort), could be deployed to calibrate, benchmark, compare and monitor credit risk associated with the bank's exposures and give indicative guidelines for credit risk management activities. Each bank may consider adopting suitable alphabetic prefixes to their rating scales, which would make their individual ratings scale distinct and unique.

2.4.2 Number of Grades used in the CRF

The number of grades used in the CRF depends on the anticipated spread in the credit quality of the exposures taken by the bank. This, in turn, is dependent on the present and the future business profile of the bank and the anticipated level of specialisation/diversification in the credit portfolio. CRFs with a large number of levels/ grades on the rating scale are, as evident, more expensive to operate as the costs of additional information for (very) fine gradation of credit-quality increase sharply. A bank can initiate the risk-grading activity on a relative smaller/ narrower scale and introduce new categories as the risk-gradation improves.

2.4.3 Key Outputs of the CRF

a. The calibration on the rating scale is expected to define the pricing and related terms and conditions for the accepted credit exposures. It is possible to define broad pricing bands and directly link the band with the calibration on the rating scale. Further refinement in the pricing proposal would be based on the bank's judgement of the prominent elements of the loan proposal and the relationship with the borrower.

b. In addition to the pricing-related decisions, the calibration on the rating scale would allow prescription of limits on the maximum quantum of exposure permissible for any credit proposal. The quantum (or amount of facility sanctioned) would depend on the credit-score on the CRF. These limits could be linked to an internal parameter (viz. a certain percentage of bank's capital funds) or could be linked to an external parameter (viz. a certain percentage of the total debt required by the borrower). This would help in a larger dispersion of risk amongst lenders and limit risk concentration in moderate credit-quality projects.

c. The rating scale could also be used for deciding on the tenure of the proposed assistance.

d. The rating scale could also be used to decide on the frequency/intensity of monitoring of the exposure. Banks may also use the rating scale to keep a close track of deteriorating credit quality and decide on the remedial measures which the deterioration may warrant. For instance, the frequency of surveillance on category 5 exposures could be kept at quarterly intervals, while those on category 3 loans could be half-yearly. More importantly, movement of an existing exposure to the "unacceptable" category of credit risk (grades 6 to 9) should directly identify the extent of provisioning (loan loss reserves) that need to be earmarked for expected losses.

e. Though loss-provisions are often specified by the regulator (e.g. the RBI provisioning norms), banks should develop their own internal norms and maintain a certain level of "reasonable over-provisioning" as a best practice. Specifically, while the credit exposure/asset is clearly facing rapid/steady erosion and is on the downhill transition path, anticipatory provisioning can be done based on the calibrations on the risk-rating scale. These provisions could be in the nature of general provisions.

2.5 Operating Design of the CRF

2.5.1 Which Exposures are Rated?

The first element of the operating design is to determine which exposures are required to be rated through the CRF. There may be a case for size-based classification of exposures and linking the risk-rating process to these size-based categories. The shortcoming of this arrangement is that though significant credit migration/deterioration/erosion occurs in the smaller-sized exposures, these are not captured by the CRF. In addition, the size-criteria are also linked with the tenure-criteria for an exposure. In several instances, large-sized exposures over a short tenure may not require the extent of surveillance and credit monitoring that is required for a smaller sized long-tenure exposure. Given this apparent lack of clarity, a policy of **'all exposures are to be rated'** should be followed.

2.5.2 The Risk-Rating Process

The credit approval process within the bank is expected to replicate the flow of analysis/appraisal of credit-risk calibration on the CRF. As indicated above the CRF may be designed in such a way that the risk rating has certain linkages with the amount, tenure and pricing of exposure. These default linkages may be either specified upfront or may be developed with empirical details over a period of time. The risk rating assigned to each credit proposal would thus directly lead into the related decisions of acceptance (or rejection), amount, tenure and pricing of the (accepted) proposal.

For each proposal, the credit/risk staff would assign a rating and forward the recommendation to the higher level of the credit selection process. The proposed risk rating is either reaffirmed or re-calibrated at the time of final credit approval and sanction. Any revisions that may become necessary in the risk-ratings are utilised to upgrade the CRF system and the operating guidelines. In this manner, the CRF maintains its "incremental upgradation" feature and changes in the lending environment are captured by the system. The risk-rating process would be equally relevant in the credit-monitoring/surveillance stage. All changes in the underlying credit-quality are calibrated on the risk-scale and corresponding remedial actions are initiated.

2.5.3 Assigning & Monitoring Risk-Ratings

In conventional banks, the practice of segregating the "relationship management" and the "credit appraisal" functions is quite prevalent. One of the variants of this arrangement is that responsibilities for calibration on the risk-rating scale are divided between the "relationship" and the "credit" groups. All large-sized exposures (above a limit) are appraised independently by the "credit" group. Generally, the activities of assigning and approving risk-ratings need to be segregated. Though the front-office or conventional relationship staff can assign the risk-ratings, the responsibilities of final approval and monitoring should be vested with a separate credit staff.

2.5.4 Mechanism of Arriving at Risk-Ratings

The risk ratings, as specified above, are collective readings on the pre-specified scale and reflect the underlying credit-risk for a prospective exposure. The CRF could be separate for relatively peculiar businesses like banking, finance companies, real-estate developers, etc. For all industries (manufacturing sector), a common CRF may be used. The peculiarity of a particular industry can be captured by assigning different weights to aspects like entry barriers, access to technology, ability of new entrants to access raw materials, etc. The following stepwise activities outline the indicative process for arriving at risk-ratings.

Step I	Identify all the principal business and financial risk elements
Step II	Allocate weights to principal risk components
Step III	Compare with weights given in similar sectors and check for consistency
Step IV	Establish the key parameters (sub-components of the principal risk elements)
Step V	Assign weights to each of the key parameters
Step VI	Rank the key parameters on the specified scale
Step VII	Arrive at the credit-risk rating on the CRF
Step VIII	Compare with previous risk-ratings of similar exposures and check for consistency
Step IX	Conclude the credit-risk calibration on the CRF

The risk-rating process would represent collective decision making principles and, as indicated above, would involve some in-built arrangements for ensuring the consistency of the output. The rankings would be largely comparative. As a bank's perception of the exposure improves/changes during the course of the appraisal, it may be necessary to adjust the weights and the rankings given to specific risk-parameters in the CRF. Such changes would be deliberated and the arguments for substantiating these adjustments would be clearly communicated in the appraisal documents.

2.5.5 Standardisation and Benchmarks for Risk-Ratings

In a lending environment dominated by industrial and corporate credits, the assignors of risk-ratings utilise benchmarks or pre-specified standards for assessing the risk profile of a potential borrower. These standards usually consist of financial ratios and credit-migration statistics, which capture the financial risks faced by the potential borrower (e.g. operating and financial leverage, profitability, liquidity, debt-servicing ability, etc.). The business risks associated with an exposure (e.g. cyclicality of industry, threats of product or technology substitution etc.) are also addressed in the CRF. The output of the credit-appraisal process, specifically the financial ratios, is directly compared with the specified benchmarks for a particular risk category. In these cases, the risk rating is fairly standardised and CRF allocates a grade or a numeric value for the overall risk profile of the proposed exposure.

The industrial credit environment permits a significantly higher level of benchmarking and standardisation, specifically in reference to calibration of financial risks associated with credit exposures. For all prominent industry-categories, any lender can compile profitability, leverage and debt-servicing details and utilise these to develop internal benchmarks for the CRF. As evident, developing such benchmarks and risk-standards for a portfolio of project finance exposures, as in the case of the bank, would be an altogether diverse exercise.

The CRF may also use qualitative/subjective factors in the credit decisions. Such factors are both internal and

Illustration

The CRF may specify that for the risk-rating exercise:

If Gross Revenues are between Rs.800 to Rs.1000 crore	assign a score of 2
If Operating Margin is 20% or more	assign a score of 2
If Return on Capital Employed (ROCE) is 25% or more	assign a score of 1
If Debt : Equity is between 0.60 and 0.80	assign a score of 2
If interest cover is 3.50 or more	assign a score of 1
If Debt Service Coverage Ratio (DSCR) is 1.80 or more	assign a score of 1

The next step would be to assign weights to these risk-parameters. In an industrial credit environment, the CRF may place higher weights on size (as captured in gross revenues), profitability of operations (operating margins), financial leverage (debt:equity) and debt-servicing ability (interest cover). Assume that the CRF assigns a 20% weightage to each of these four parameters and the ROCE and DSCR are given a 10% weightage each. The weighted-average score for the financial risk of the proposed exposure is 1.40, which would correspond with the extremely low risk/highest safety level-category of the CRF (category 1). Similarly, the business and the management risk of the proposed exposure are assessed and an overall/comprehensive risk rating is assigned.

external to the company. Internal factors could include integrity and quality of management of the borrower, quality of inventories/receivables and the ability of borrowers to raise finance from other sources. External factors would include views on the economy and industry such as growth prospects, technological change and options.

2.5.6 Written Communications and Formality of Procedure

The two critical aspects of the formality of procedure in the risk-rating process are:

(i) the process-flow through which a credit-transaction would flow across various units; and

(ii) the written communication on the risk-ratings assigned to a particular proposal.

The process-flow required for the credit appraisal exercise, may be explicitly drafted and communicated. It may clearly identify the transactions and linkages between various operating units of the bank.

The above discussion broadly presents some of the essential dimensions in the design of a CRF by banks. These details are indicative of the scope of work required for the CRF. Banks may make appropriate modifications to suit their requirements.

2.6 CRFs and aggregation of Credit-Risk

Analysing exposures using the CRF technique would highlight the spread (or frequency-distribution) of the credit-risk in the bank's asset portfolio and would give an indication for its future asset build-up efforts. This section briefly covers some aspects of portfolio credit-risk management, a process which would possibly be facilitated by implementing the CRF.

2.6.1 Portfolio Surveillance and Reporting

The conventional internal MIS of a bank would identify the problem-loans in the asset portfolio, as per the guidelines given by the regulator (i.e. the asset-classification guidelines of RBI). These details, however, represent only a component of the credit-risks accumulated in the asset portfolio of a bank. The CRF can be used for informing the top management on the frequency distribution of assets across the risk-rating scale, the extent of migration in the past (e.g. movement of exposures from higher to lower risk-categories or vice-versa) and the anticipated developments in the aggregated credit portfolio. The senior management may benefit from such outputs in terms of steering the organisation through various risk-cycles (e.g. initial low-risk low-return phase to consolidation and further to an incremental rise in relatively high-risk high-return exposures).

2.6.2 Adequate Levels of Provisioning for Credit Events

The spread of the asset portfolio across the risk-rating scale and the trends in rating migration would allow the bank management to determine the level of provisioning required, in addition to the regulatory minimum, to absorb unanticipated erosions in the credit quality of the assets. In most cases, provisions for loan-losses are based on the prevailing regulatory and accounting directives. However, the management may find merit in a certain prudent level of "over-provisioning". This exercise may add stability and resilience to the capital adequacy and profitability of the bank.

The extent of provisioning required could be estimated from the Expected Loss on Default [which is a product of the Probability of Default (PD) and Loss Given Default (LGD)]. Since these probabilities can be assigned only after significant empirical details are available, an alternative would be to adopt a policy of allocating/provisioning an amount which may be a proportion of the aggregate exposures in the risk-rating scale which reflect the likelihood of the assets slipping into the NPA category.

2.6.3 Guidelines for Asset Build-up, Aggregate Profitability and Pricing

As discussed earlier, a clear analysis of the prevailing risk-posture of the bank, facilitated by the CRF, would give strong recommendations for future asset build-up and business development activities. The extent of provisioning would be based on actual and anticipated erosion in credit quality and would define the "cost" of maintaining an exposure in the bank's credit portfolio. A similar analysis could be undertaken for a specific credit-product and the risk-adjusted return can be assessed. This will involve an analysis of the pricing-decisions, provisioning requirements, loss on default and the incremental impact on a bank's profitability.

2.6.4 Interaction with External Credit Assessment Institutions (ECAI)

The benefits of such a CRF system, in addition to those described above, could include a more amenable interaction with rating agencies and regulatory bodies. As regards investment ratings, the parameters laid down in para 4.1 of the Risk Management Guidelines issued by RBI in October, 1999 may be followed, i.e., the proposals for investments should also be subjected to the same degree of credit risk analysis as any loan proposals. The proposals should be subjected to detailed appraisal and a rating framework that factors in financial and non-financial parameters of issuers, sensitivity to external developments, etc. The maximum exposure to a customer should be bank-wide and include all exposures assumed by the Credit and Treasury Departments. The coupon on non-sovereign papers should be commensurate with their risk profile. The banks should exercise due caution, particularly in investment proposals, which are not rated and should ensure comprehensive risk evaluation. There should be greater interaction between Credit and Treasury Departments and the portfolio analysis should also cover the total exposures, including investments. The rating migration of the issuers and the consequent diminution in the portfolio quality should also be tracked at periodic intervals.

Credit Risk Models

3.1 A credit risk model seeks to determine, directly or indirectly, the answer to the following question: Given our past experience and our assumptions about the future, what is the present value of a given loan or fixed income security? A credit risk model would also seek to determine the (quantifiable) risk that the promised cash flows will not be forthcoming. The techniques for measuring credit risk that have evolved over the last twenty years are prompted by these questions and dynamic changes in the loan market.

3.1.1 The increasing importance of credit risk modelling should be seen as the consequence of the following three factors:

- Banks are becoming increasingly quantitative in their treatment of credit risk.
- New markets are emerging in credit derivatives and the marketability of existing loans is increasing through securitisation/loan sales market.
- Regulators are concerned to improve the current system of bank capital requirements especially as it relates to credit risk.

3.1.2 Credit Risk Models have assumed importance because they provide the decision maker with insight or knowledge that would not otherwise be readily available or that could be marshalled at prohibitive cost. In a marketplace where margins are fast disappearing and the pressure to lower pricing is unrelenting, models give their users a competitive edge. The credit risk models are intended to aid banks in quantifying, aggregating and managing risk across geographical and product lines. The outputs of these models also play increasingly important roles in banks' risk management and performance measurement processes, customer profitability analysis, risk-based pricing, active portfolio management and capital structure decisions. Credit risk modelling may result in better internal risk management and may have the potential to be used in the supervisory oversight of banking organisations.

3.2 In the measurement of credit risk, models may be classified mainly along **two different dimensions**: the techniques employed and the domain of applications in the credit process.

3.2.1 **Techniques**: The following are the more commonly used techniques:

(a) **Econometric Techniques** such as linear and multiple discriminant analysis, multiple regression, logic analysis and probability of default, etc.

(b) **Neural networks** are computer-based systems that use the same data employed in the econometric techniques but arrive at the decision model using alternative implementations of a trial and error method.

(c) **Optimisation models** are mathematical programming techniques that discover the optimum weights for borrower and loan attributes that minimise lender error and maximise profits.

(d) **Rule-based or expert systems** are characterised by a set of decision rules, a knowledge base consisting of data such as industry financial ratios, and a structured inquiry process to be used by the analyst in obtaining the data on a particular borrower.

(e) **Hybrid Systems:** In these systems simulation are driven in part by a direct causal relationship, the parameters of which are determined through estimation techniques.

3.2.2 Domain of application: These models are used in a variety of domains:

(a) **Credit approval**: Models are used on a stand-alone basis or in conjunction with a judgemental override system for approving credit in the consumer lending business. The use of such models has expanded to include small business lending. They are generally not used in approving large corporate loans, but they may be one of the inputs to a decision.

(b) **Credit rating determination**: Quantitative models are used in deriving 'shadow bond rating' for unrated securities and commercial loans. These ratings, in turn, influence portfolio limits and other lending limits used by the institution. In some instances, the credit rating predicted by the model is used within an institution to challenge the rating assigned by the traditional credit analysis process.

(c) Credit risk models may be used to suggest the **risk premia** that should be charged in view of the probability of loss and the size of the loss given default. Using a mark-to-market model, an institution may evaluate the costs and benefits of holding a financial asset. Unexpected losses implied by a credit model may be used to set the capital charge in pricing.

(d) **Early warning**: Credit models are used to flag potential problems in the portfolio to facilitate early corrective action.

(e) **Common credit language**: Credit models may be used to select assets from a pool to construct a portfolio acceptable to investors at the time of asset securitisation or to achieve the minimum credit quality needed to obtain the desired credit rating. Underwriters may use such models for due diligence on the portfolio (such as a collateralised pool of commercial loans).

(f) **Collection strategies**: Credit models may be used in deciding on the best collection or workout strategy to pursue. If, for example, a credit model indicates that a borrower is experiencing short-term liquidity problems rather than a decline in credit fundamentals, then an appropriate workout may be devised.

3.3 Credit Risk Models: Approaches

3.3.1 The literature on quantitative risk modelling has two different approaches to credit risk measurement. The first approach is the development of statistical models through analysis of historical data. This approach was frequently used in the last two decades. The second type of modelling approach tries to capture distribution of the firm's asset-value over a period of time.

3.3.2 The statistical approach tries to rate the firms on a discrete or continuous scale. The linear model introduced by Altman (1967), also known as the Z-score Model, separates defaulting firms from non-defaulting ones on the basis of certain financial ratios. Altman, Hartzell, and Peck (1995,1996) have modified the original Z-score model to develop a model specific to emerging markets. This model is known as the Emerging Market Scoring (EMS) model.

3.3.3 The second type of modelling approach tries to capture distribution of the firm's asset-value over a period of time. This model is based on the expected default frequency (EDF) model. It calculates the asset value of a firm from the market value of its equity using an option pricing based approach that recognises equity as a call option on the underlying asset of the firm. It tries to estimate the asset value path of the firm over a time horizon. The default risk is the probability of the estimated asset value falling below a pre-specified default point. This model is based conceptually on Merton's (1974) contingent claim framework and has been working very well for estimating default risk in a liquid market.

3.3.4 Closely related to credit risk models are **portfolio risk models**. In the last three years, important advances have been made in modelling credit risk in lending portfolios. The new models are designed to quantify credit risk on a portfolio basis, and thus are applied at the time of diversification as well as portfolio-based pricing. These models estimate the loss distribution associated with the portfolio and identify the risky components by assessing the risk contribution of each member in the portfolio.

3.4 Banks may adopt any model depending on their size, complexity, risk-bearing capacity and risk appetite, etc. However, the credit risk models followed by banks should, at the least, achieve the following:

- ❖ Result in differentiating the degree of credit risk in different credit exposures of a bank. The system could provide for transaction-based or borrower-based rating or both. It is recommended that all exposures be rated. Restricting risk measurement to only large-sized exposures may fail to capture the portfolio risk in entirety for a variety of reasons. For instance, a large-sized exposure for a short time may be less risky than a small-sized exposure for a long time.

- ❖ Identify concentration in the portfolios.

- ❖ Identify problem credits before they become NPAs.

- ❖ Identify adequacy/inadequacy of loan provisions.

- ❖ Help in pricing of credit.
- ❖ Recognise variations in macro-economic factors and a possible impact under alternative scenarios.
- ❖ Determine the impact on profitability of transactions and relationship.

Portfolio Management and Risk Limits

4.1 The need for credit portfolio management emanates from the necessity to optimize the benefits associated with diversification and reduce the potential adverse impact of concentration of exposures to a particular borrower, sector or industry. The conventional approach to credit portfolio management has been largely based on the counter-party exposure limits, which largely provides the guideline for incremental asset/exposure build-up. This "forward" or incremental approach to credit portfolio management is, to an extent, a reactive strategy and though it does guide the decision-making process, it has limited contribution for managing the existing credit portfolio of the bank.

4.2 The recent developments in the measurement and management of portfolio credit risk have been based on two key attributes: ***correlation*** and ***volatility***. Consider two companies, one operates large capacities in the steel sector and the other a large player in the cement sector, promoted by two entirely unrelated promoters. Though these would classify as two separate counter-parties, both of them may be highly sensitive to the Government's expenditure in new projects/investments. Thus, a reduction in Government investments could impact these two companies simultaneously (correlation), impacting the credit-quality of such a portfolio (volatility), even though from a regulatory or conventional perspective, the risk had been diversified (two separate promoters, two separate industries). Thus, though the credit portfolio may be well diversified and fulfill the prescribed criteria for counter-party exposure limits, the high correlation in potential performance between two counter-parties may impact the portfolio quality (default levels) under stress conditions.

4.3 In addition to the widespread instances of high correlation and resultant volatility, the emergence of new techniques for managing a bank's credit portfolio have actively contributed to the development and adoption of broader credit risk management practices. Specifically, the adoption and wider acceptance of securitisation of loan assets in the developed markets has permitted banks to pursue credit portfolio management on a proactive manner. These have usually been in the nature of collateralised loan obligations. Though securitisation of loan receivables, mainly consumer and auto loans, has been prevalent in India, it has usually been deployed as an asset acquisition or a hive-off approach rather than active credit portfolio management. The steps taken to enhance the liquidity and depth of debt markets in India and simplify the process of securitisation are expected to improve the prospects of credit portfolio management in the near future.

4.4 The measurement of credit-portfolio concentration has been elaborated in detail in the regulatory prescriptions for counter-party exposures in India. The issue of credit portfolio correlation is discussed here in some detail. In statistical terms, credit portfolio correlation would mean the number of times companies/counter-parties in a portfolio defaulted simultaneously. As evident, this analysis is impossible in practice and the number of such instances for developing a reasonable generalisation would be too few. Some credit portfolio management techniques developed overseas estimate the correlation between defaults and bond-market spreads and generalise this for assessing the correlation in a given portfolio. Given the limited data on corporate bond market spreads and their statistical linkages with ratings in India, this approach may not be appropriate for Indian banks at this stage. Banks should, however, direct their data management efforts in this direction so that a beginning in active portfolio management can be made.

4.5 One possible technique for analysing credit-portfolio correlation is based on a macro-economic factor model. This approach involves projecting the performance (volatility) of a credit portfolio under altering macro-economic environments. In specific terms, this would involve a stress-test on the debt-servicing ability of a portfolio of borrowers under alternative scenarios. The input data would consist of the projected financial performance (income statement and balance sheet details) of each of these portfolio constituents. In the appraisal system adopted by Indian banks in general, these are normally developed for individual borrowers for seeking credit approvals from the specific internal authorities. Such portfolio constituents could be relatively independent counter-parties, spanning a relatively wide spectrum of region, industry, size of operation, adoption of technology and promoters. The key financial parameters of these counterparties (growth, profitability, access to funds, etc.) should be linked to the macro-economic parameters under consideration. Some of the relevant macro-economic parameters could include overall growth rates, growth in exports/industrial/agricultural sectors, interest rates, exchange rates, import duties, equity market and liquidity conditions. By developing alternative scenarios for these parameters, the credit-portfolio's aggregate performance (default rates and levels) can be assessed and possible correlation between a set of obligors (even though they constitute entirely separate counter-parties) may be established. For instance, under the assumptions of low overall economic growth, poor growth in agriculture sector and reduction in import duties, the assessment may give some correlation between the borrowers in the petro-chemicals industry and the consumer-electronics industry. Though there may not be any "counter party" relationship in this set of borrowers, both of them are possibly susceptible to reduced import duties and low economic growth. These illustrations are relatively simplistic and the detailed analysis, as discussed above, may give critical inputs for minimising the credit risk of the given portfolio. A possible advantage of starting with the macro-economic factor model is that it is amenable to the current levels of credit risk assessment practices in Indian banks and can be correspondingly adopted with relative ease. Though superior and more sophisticated tools have been developed, their findings may be limited due to the lack of representative data. Such options can be considered as Indian banks further enhance their internal systems and processes in credit risk management.

Managing Credit Risk in Inter-bank Exposures

5.1 During the course of its business, a bank may assume exposures on other banks, arising from trade transactions, money placements for liquidity management purposes, hedging, trading and transactional banking services such as clearing and custody, etc. Such transactions entail a credit risk, as defined, and therefore, it is important that a proper credit evaluation of the banks is undertaken. It must cover both the interpretation of the bank's financial statements as well as forming a judgement on non-financial areas such as management, ownership, peer/market perception and country factors.

5.2 The key financial parameters to be evaluated for any bank are:

a) Capital Adequacy
b) Asset Quality
c) Liquidity
d) Profitability

Banks will normally have access to information available publicly to assess the credit risk posed by the counter-party bank.

5.2.1 Capital Adequacy

5.2.1.1 Banks with high capital ratios above the regulatory minimum levels, particularly Tier I, will be assigned a high rating whereas banks with low ratios well below the standards and with low ability to access capital will be at the other end of the spectrum.

5.2.1.2 Capital adequacy needs to be appropriate to the size and structure of the balance sheet as it represents the buffer to absorb losses during difficult times. Over-capitalization can impact overall profitability. Related to the issue of capitalization, is also the ability to raise fresh capital as and when required. Publicly-listed banks and state-owned banks may be best positioned to raise capital whilst the unlisted private banks or regional banks are dependent entirely on the wealth and/or credibility of their owners.

5.2.1.3 The capital adequacy ratio is normally indicated in the published audited accounts. In addition, it will be useful to calculate the Capital to Total Assets ratio which indicates the owners' share in the assets of the business. The ratio of Tier I capital to Total Assets represents the extent to which the bank can absorb a counter-party collapse. Tier I capital is not owed to anyone and is available to cover possible losses. It has no maturity or repayment requirement, and is expected to remain a permanent component of the counter-party's capital.

5.2.1.4 The Basel standards currently require banks to have a capital adequacy ratio of 8% with Tier I ratio not less than 4%. The Reserve Bank of India requirement is 9%. The Basel Committee is planning to introduce the New Capital Accord and these requirements could change the dimension of the capital of banks.

5.2.2 Asset Quality

5.2.2.1 The asset portfolio in its entirety should be evaluated and should include an assessment of both funded items and off-balance sheet items. Whilst non-performing assets and provisioning ratios will reflect the quality of the loan book, high volatility of valuations and earnings will reflect exposure to the capital market and sensitive sectors.

The key ratios to be analysed are

- Gross NPAs to Gross Advances ratio,
- Net NPAs to Net Advances ratio
- Provisions Held to Gross Advances ratio and
- Provisions Held to Gross NPAs ratio.

5.2.2.2 Some issues which should be taken cognisance of, and which require further critical examination are:

— where exposure to a particular sector is above a certain level, say, 10% of total assets

— where a significant part of the portfolio is to counter-parties based in countries which are considered to be very risky

— where Net NPAs are above a certain level, say, 5% of the loan assets.

— where loan loss provision is less than a certain level, say, 50% of the Gross NPA.

— where high risk/return lending accounts for the

majority of the assets.

— where there are rapid rates of loan growth. (These can be a precursor to reducing asset quality as periods of rapid expansion are often followed by slowdowns which make the bank vulnerable.)

— net impact of mark-to-market values of treasury transactions.

5.2.2.3 Commercial banks are increasingly venturing into investment banking activities where asset considerations additionally focus on the marketability of the assets, as well as the quality of the instruments. Preferably banks should mark-to-market their entire investment portfolio and treat sticky investments as "non-performing", which should also be adequately provided for.

5.2.3 Liquidity

5.2.3.1 Commercial bank deposits generally have a much shorter contractual maturity than loans, and liquidity management needs to provide a cushion to cover anticipated deposit withdrawals. The key ratios to be analysed are

- Total Liquid Assets to Total Assets ratio (the higher the ratio the more liquid the bank is).
- Total Liquid Assets to Total Deposits ratio (this measures the bank's ability to meet withdrawals).
- Loans to Deposits ratio.
- Inter-bank deposits to total deposits ratio.

5.2.3.2 It is necessary to develop an appropriate level of correlation between assets and liabilities. Account should be taken of the extent to which borrowed funds are required to bolster capital and the respective redemption profiles.

5.2.4 Profitability

5.2.4.1 A consistent year on year growth in profitability is required to provide an acceptable return to shareholders and retain resources to fund future growth. The key ratios to be analysed are:

- Return on Average Assets (measures a bank's growth/decline in profits in comparison with its balance sheet expansion/contraction).
- Return on Equity (provides an indication of how well the bank is performing for its owners).
- Net Interest Margin (measures the difference between interest paid and interest earned, and therefore a bank's ability to earn interest income).
- Operating Expenses to Net Revenue ratio (the cost/income ratio of the bank).

5.2.4.2 The degree of reliance upon interest income compared with fees earned, heavy dependency on certain sectors, and the sustainability of income streams are relevant factors to be borne in mind.

5.2.4.3 The ability of a bank to analyse another bank on the above lines will depend upon the information available publicly and also the strength of disclosures in the financial statements.

5.3 In addition to the quantitative indices, other key parameters to be assessed are:

- Ownership
- Management ability
- Peer comparison/Market perception
- Country of incorporation/Regulatory environment

5.3.1 ***Ownership***

The spread and nature of the ownership structure is important, as it impinges on the propensity to induct additional capital. Support from a large body of shareholders is difficult to obtain if the bank's performance is adverse, whilst a smaller shareholder base constrains the ability to garner funds.

5.3.2 **Management Ability**

Frequent changes in senior management, change in a key figure, and the lack of succession planning need to be viewed with suspicion. Risk management is a key indicator of the management's ability as it is integral to the health of any institution. Risk management should be deeply embedded and respected in the culture of the financial institution.

5.3.3 **Peer Comparison/Market Perception**

It is recognised that balance sheets tend to show different structures from one country to another, and from one type of bank to another. Accordingly, it is appropriate to assess a bank's financial statements against those of its comparable peers. Similarly market sentiment is highly important to a bank's ability to maintain an adequate funding base, but is not necessarily reflective of published information. Special notice should be taken where the overall performance of the peer sector, in general, falls below international standards.

5.3.4 Country of Incorporation/Regulatory Environment

Country risk needs to be evaluated since a bank which is financially strong may not be permitted to meet its commitments in view of the regulatory environment or the financial state of the country in which it is operating in.

5.4 Banks should be rated (called Bank Tierings) on the basis of the above factors. An indicative tiering scale is:[1]

Bank Tier	Description
1	Low risk
2	Modest risk
3	Satisfactory risk
4	Fair risk
5	Acceptable risk
6	Watch list
7	Substandard
8	Doubtful
9	Loss

5.5 Facilities

Facilities to banks can be classified into three categories:

[1] The rating scale for bank rating should be in tandem with CRF to synthesise credit risk on account of all activities for the bank as a whole.

a) On-balance sheet items such as cash advances, bond holdings and investments, and off-balance sheet items which are not subject to market fluctuation risk such as guarantees, acceptances and letters of credit.

b) Facilities which are off-balance sheet and subject to market fluctuation risk such as foreign exchange and derivative products.

c) Settlement facilities: These cover risks arising through payment systems or through settlement of treasury and securities transactions.

The tiering system enables a bank to establish internal parameters to help determine acceptable limits of exposure to a particular bank/banking group. These parameters should be used to determine the maximum level of (a) and (b) above, maximum tenors for term products which may be considered prudent for a bank and settlement limits. Medium term loan facilities and standby facilities should be sanctioned very exceptionally. Standby lines, by their very nature, are likely to be drawn only at a time when the risk in making funds available is generally perceived to be unattractive.

Bank-wise exposure limits should be set taking into account the counter-party and country risks. The credit risk management of exposure to banks should be centralised on a bank-wide basis.

Credit Risk in Off-balance Sheet Exposures

Risk Identification and Assessment of Limits

6.1 *Credit risk in non-fund based business of banks need to be assessed in a manner similar to the assessment of fund-based business since it has the potential to become a funded liability in case the customer is not able to meet his commitments. Financial guarantees are generally long-term in nature, and assessment of these requirements should be similar to the evaluation of requests for term loans. As contracts are generally for a term of 2-3 years, banks must obtain cash flows over this time horizon, arising from the specific contract they intend to support, and determine the viability of financing the contract.*

Risk Monitoring and Control

6.2 *For reducing credit risk on account of such off-balance sheet exposures, banks may adopt a variety of measures some of which are indicated below:*

i) Banks must ensure that the security, which is available to the funded lines, also covers the LC lines and the guarantee facilities. On some occasions, it will be appropriate to take a charge over the fixed assets as well, especially in the case of long-term guarantees.

ii) In the case of guarantees covering contracts, banks must ensure that the clients have the requisite technical skills and experience to execute the contracts. The value of the contracts must be determined on a case-by-case basis, and separate limits should be set up for each contract. The progress vis-à-vis physical and financial indicators should be monitored regularly, and any slippages should be highlighted in the credit review.

iii) The strategy to sanction non-fund facilities with a view to increase earnings should be properly balanced vis-à-vis the risk involved and extended only after a thorough assessment of credit risk is undertaken.

Country Risk

7.1 ***Country risk*** is the possibility that a country will be unable to service or repay its debts to foreign lenders in a timely manner. In banking, this risk arises on account of cross-border lending and investment. The risk manifests itself either in **the inability** or **the unwillingness** of the obligor to meet its liability.

Country risk comprises of the following risks:

- ***Transfer risk,*** which is the core risk under country risk, arises on account of the possibility of losses due to restrictions on external remittances. Consequently, an obligor may be able to pay in local currency, but may not be able to pay in foreign currency. This type of risk may occur when foreign exchange shortages either close or restrict a country's cross-border foreign exchange market.

- ***Sovereign risk*** is associated with lending to government of a sovereign nation or to taking government guarantees. The risk lies in the fact that sovereign entities may claim immunity from the legal process or might not abide by a judgement, and it might prove impossible to secure redress through legal action. Ordinarily, it is assumed that there will be no default by a sovereign. This, however, does not mean that there is no risk involved in sovereign lending, for the risk may manifest itself in terms of rehabilitation of an indebted country in terms of financial solvency and liquidity for which there may be rescheduling of country debt or external debt.

- ***Non-sovereign or political risk*** arises when the political environment or legislative process of a country leads to the Government taking over the assets of the financial entity (e.g. nationalisation) and preventing discharge of its liabilities in a manner that had been agreed to. It is also referred to as risk of appropriation and expropriation. Non-sovereign risk includes, in addition to sovereign risk, private claims and direct investments like lending to corporates and project finance lending and includes risks associated with legal frameworks and economic environment.

- ***Cross-border risk*** arises on account of the borrower being a resident of a country other than the country where the cross-border asset is booked, and includes exposures to local residents denominated in currencies other than the local currency.

- ***Currency risk*** is the possibility that exchange rate changes will alter the expected amount of principal and return of the lending or investment. At times, banks may try to cope with this specific risk on the lending side by shifting the risk associated with exchange rate fluctuations to the borrowers. The risk however does not get extinguished, but gets converted to credit risk.

- ***Macroeconomic and Structural Fragility Risk*** has

come into prominence after the East Asian crises of the 1990s. In these crises firms could purchase foreign exchange to service foreign debt but the collapse of exchange rates and the surge in interest rates due to severe government restrictions on firms owning external debt resulted in highly unfavourable exchange rates and very high interest costs on domestic borrowings for these firms. This severely impaired these firms' ability to service foreign debt. The structural fragility risk can also include that associated with poor development of domestic bankruptcy laws and weak courts for their enforcement.

7.2 Broad Contours of Country Risk Management (CRM)

The broad contours of CRM are:

- Risk Categories
- Country Risk Assessments
- Fixing of country limits
- Monitoring of country exposures

7.2.1 Risk Categories

Countries can be broadly classified into six risk categories —insignificant, low, moderate, high, very high and off-credit. IBA **would be assigned the responsibility of developing a mechanism for assigning countries to the six risk categories specified above.** Banks may be allowed to adopt a more conservative categorisation of the countries.

7.2.2 Country Risk (CR) Assessment

To begin with, banks may adopt the sovereign ratings of

international credit rating agencies. However, banks should eventually put in place appropriate systems to move over to internal assessment of country risk within a prescribed period, say by 31 March 2005. Banks may adopt the ratings of any of the international credit rating agencies during the transition period. In case there is divergence in the ratings accorded to any country by the international credit rating agencies, banks may adopt the lower/lowest of the ratings.

Banks should also evolve sound systems for measuring and monitoring country risk. The system should be able to identify the full dimensions of country risk as well as incorporating features that acknowledge the links between credit and market risk. Banks should use a variety of internal and external sources as a means to measure country risk. Banks should not rely solely on rating agencies or other external sources as their only country risk-monitoring tool. Banks should also incorporate information from the relevant country managers of their foreign branches into their country risk assessments. However, the rating accorded by a bank to any country should not be better than the rating of that country by the international rating agency.

The frequency of periodic reviews of country risk ratings should be at least once a year with a provision to review the rating of specific country, based on any major events in that country, where bank exposure is high, even before the next periodical review of the ratings is due.

7.2.4 Fixing of country limits

Bank Boards may set country exposure limits in relation to the bank's regulatory capital (Tier I + Tier II) with sub-limits, if considered necessary, for products, branches, maturity etc. The basis for setting the limits for the country/ category shall be left to the discretion of the banks' Boards. The country exposure limits set by the Board should be reviewed periodically.

The exposure limit for any country should not exceed its regulatory capital, except in the case of the insignificant risk category. In respect of foreign banks, the regulatory capital would be the capital held in their Indian books.

Banks may also set up regional exposure limits for country groups, at the discretion of their Boards. The Board may decide on the basis for grouping of countries and also lay down the guidelines regarding all aspects of such regional exposure limits.

7.2.5 Monitoring of country exposures

Banks should monitor their country exposures on a weekly basis before switching over to real-time monitoring. However, exposures to high-risk (and above) categories should be monitored on a real-time basis. Banks should switch-over to real-time monitoring of country exposures (all categories) by 31 March 2004.

Boards should review the country risk exposures at every

meeting. The review should include progress in establishing internal country rating systems, compliance with the regulatory and the internal limits, results of stress tests and the exit options available to the banks in respect of countries belonging to 'high risk & above' categories.

Management of country risk should incorporate stress testing as one method to monitor actual and potential risks. Stress testing should include an assessment of the impact of alternative outcomes to important underlying assumptions.

Country risk management processes employed by banks would require adequate internal controls that include audits or other appropriate overseeing mechanisms to ensure the integrity of the information used by senior officials in overseeing compliance with policies and limits.

Loan Review Mechanism/Credit Audit

Credit Audit examines compliance with existing sanction and post-sanction processes/procedures laid down by the bank from time to time.

8.1 Objectives of Credit Audit

- Improvement in the quality of the credit portfolio.
- Review the sanction process and compliance status of large loans.
- Feedback on regulatory compliance.
- Independent review of Credit Risk Assessment.
- Pick up early warning signals and suggest remedial measures.
- Recommend corrective action to improve credit quality, credit administration and credit skills of staff, etc.

8.2 Structure of Credit Audit Department

The credit audit/loan review mechanism may be assigned to a specific department or the Inspection and Audit Department.

8.3 Functions of the Credit Audit Department

- To process Credit Audit Reports.
- To analyse Credit Audit findings and advise the departments/functionaries concerned.
- To follow up with controlling authorities.
- To apprise the Top Management.
- To process the responses received and arrange for closure of the relative Credit Audit Reports.

➢ To maintain a database of advances subjected to Credit Audit.

8.4 Scope and Coverage

The focus of credit audit needs to be broadened from the account level to look at the overall portfolio and the credit process being followed. The important areas are:

8.4.1 Portfolio Review: Examine the quality of Credit & Invest-ment (Quasi Credit) Portfolio and suggest measures for improvement, including reduction of concentrations in certain sectors to levels indicated in the Loan Policy and Prudential Limits suggested by RBI.

8.4.2 Loan Review: Review of the sanction process and status of post sanction processes/procedures (not just restricted to large accounts)

- All fresh proposals and proposals for renewal of limits (within 3-6 months from date of sanction).
- All existing accounts with sanction limits equal to or above a cut-off depending upon the size of activity.
- Randomly selected (say 5-10%) proposals from the rest of the portfolio.
- Accounts of sister concerns/group/associate concerns of above accounts, even if the limit is less than the cut-off.

8.4.3 Action Points for Review

- Verify compliance of the bank's laid down policies and regulatory compliance with regard to sanction
- Examine adequacy of documentation.

- Conduct the credit risk assessment.
- Examine the conduct of account and follow up looked at by line functionaries.
- Oversee action taken by line functionaries in respect of serious irregularities.
- Detect early warning signals and suggest remedial measures thereof.

8.4.4 Frequency of Review

The frequency of review should vary depending on the magnitude of risk (say, for high-risk accounts—3 months, for the average-risk accounts—6 months, for the low-risk accounts—1 year).

- Feedback on general regulatory compliance.
- Examine adequacy of policies, procedures and practices.
- Review the Credit Risk Assessment methodology.
- Examine reporting system and exceptions thereof.
- Recommend corrective action for credit administration and credit skills of staff.
- Forecast likely happenings in the near future.

8.5 Procedure to be followed for Credit Audit

- ➢ Credit Audit is conducted on-site, i.e. at the branch which has appraised the advance and where the main operative credit limits are made available.
- ➢ Report on the conduct of accounts of allocated limits are to be called for from the corresponding branches.
- ➢ Credit auditors are not required to visit borrowers' factory/office premises.

RAROC Pricing/Economic Profit

9.1 In acquiring assets, banks should use the pricing mechanism in conjunction with product/geography/industry/tenor limits. For example, if a bank believes that construction loans for commercial complexes are unattractive from a portfolio perspective, it can raise the price of these loans to a level that will act as a disincentive to borrowers. This is an instance of ***marginal cost pricing***—the notion that the price of an asset should compensate the institution for its marginal cost as measured on a risk-adjusted basis. Marginal cost pricing may not always work. A bank may have idle capacity and capital that has not been deployed. While such an institution clearly would not want to make a loan at a negative spread, it would probably view even a small positive spread as worthwhile as long as the added risk was acceptable.

9.2 Institutions tend to book unattractively priced loans when they are unable to allocate their cost base with clarity or to make fine differentiations of their risks. If a bank cannot allocate its costs, then it will make no distinction between the cost of lending to borrowers that require little analysis and the cost of lending to borrowers that require a considerable amount of review and follow up. Similarly, if the spread is tied to a too coarsely graded risk rating system (one, for example, with just four grades) then it is more difficult to differentiate among risks when pricing than if the risk rating is graduated over a larger scale with, say, 15 grades.

9.3 A ***cost-plus-profit pricing strategy*** will work in the short run, but in the long run borrowers will balk and start looking for alternatives. Cost-plus-profit pricing will also work when a bank has some flexibility to compete on an array of services rather than exclusively on price. The difficulties with pricing are greater in markets where the lender is a price taker rather than a price leader.

9.4 The pricing is based on the borrower's risk rating, tenor, collateral, guarantees, historic loan loss rates, and covenants. A capital charge is applied based on a hurdle rate and a capital ratio.* Using these assumptions, the rate to be charged for a loan to a customer with a given rating could be calculated.

9.5 This relatively simple approach to credit pricing works well as long as the assumptions are correct—especially those about the borrower's credit quality. This method is used in many banks today. The main drawbacks of this method are:

- Only 'expected losses' are linked to the borrower's credit quality. The capital charge based on the volatility of losses in the credit risk category may also be too small. If the loan were to default, the loss would have to be made up from income from non-defaulting loans.

- It implicitly assumes only two possible states for a loan: default or no default. It does not model the

* The hurdle rate is defined as the minimum acceptable return on a business activity.

credit risk premium or discount resulting from improvement or decline in the borrower's financial condition, which is meaningful only if the asset may be repriced or sold at par.

9.6 Banks have long struggled to find the best ways of allocating capital in a manner consistent with the risks taken. They have found it difficult to come up with a consistent and credible way of allocating capital for such varying sources of revenue as loan commitments, revolving lines of credit (which have no maturity), and secured versus unsecured lending. The different approaches for allocating capital are as under:

- One approach is to allocate capital to business units based on their asset size. Although it is true that a larger portfolio will have larger losses, this approach also means that the business unit is forced to employ all the capital allocated to it. Moreover, this method treats all risks alike.

- Another approach is to use the regulatory (risk-adjusted) capital as the allocated capital. The problem with this approach is that regulatory capital may or may not reflect the true risk of a business. For example, for regulatory purposes, a loan to an AAA rated customer requires the same amount of capital per rupee lent as one to a small business.

- Yet another approach is to use unexpected losses in a sub-portfolio (standard deviation of the annual losses taken over time) as a proxy for capital to be allocated.

The problem with this approach is that it ignores default correlations across sub-portfolios. The volatility of a sub-portfolio may in fact dampen the volatility of the institution's portfolio, so pricing decisions based on the volatility of the sub-portfolio may not be optimal. In practical terms, this means that one line of business within a lending institution may sometimes subsidize another.

Risk Adjusted Return on Capital (RAROC)

9.7 As it became clearer that banks needed to add an appropriate capital charge in the pricing process, the concept of risk adjusting the return or risk adjusting the capital arose. The value-producing capacity of an asset (or a business) is expressed as a ratio that allows comparisons to be made between assets (or businesses) of varying sizes and risk characteristics. The ratio is based either on the size of the asset or the size of the capital allocated to it. When an institution can observe asset prices directly (and/or infer risk from observable asset prices) then it can determine how much capital to hold based on the volatility of the asset. This is the essence of the mark-to-market concept. If the capital to be held is excessive relative to the total return that would be earned from the asset, then the bank will not acquire it. If the asset is already in the bank's portfolio, it will be sold. The availability of a liquid market to buy and sell these assets is a precondition for this approach. When banks talk about asset concentration and correlation, the question of capital allocation is always in the background because it is allocated capital that absorbs the potential consequences (unexpected losses) resulting from such concentration and correlation causes.

9.8 RAROC allocates a capital charge to a transaction or a line of business at an amount equal to the maximum expected loss (at a 99% confidence level) over one year on an after-tax basis. As may be expected, ***the higher the volatility of the returns, the more capital is allocated. The higher capital allocation means that the transaction has to generate cash flows large enough to offset the volatility of returns, which results from the credit risk, market risk, and other risks taken***. The RAROC process estimates the asset value that may prevail in the worst-case scenario and then equates the capital cushion to be provided for the potential loss.

9.9 RAROC is an improvement over the traditional approach in that it allows one to compare two businesses with different risk (volatility of returns) profiles. A transaction may give a higher return but at a higher risk. Using a hurdle rate (expected rate of return), a lender can also use the RAROC principle to set the target pricing on a relationship or a transaction. Although not all assets have market price distribution, RAROC is a first step toward examining an institution's entire balance sheet on a mark-to-market basis—if only to understand the risk-return trade-offs that have been made.

New Capital Accord: Implications for Credit Risk Management

10.1 The Basel Committee on Banking Supervision had released in June 1999 the first Consultative Paper on a ***New Capital Adequacy Framework*** with the intention of replacing the current broad-brush 1988 Accord. The Basel Committee has released a Second Consultative Document in January 2001, which contains refined proposals for the three pillars of the New Accord—Minimum Capital Requirements, Supervisory Review and Market Discipline.

10.2 The Committee proposes two approaches, viz., Standardised and Internal Rating Based (IRB) for estimating regulatory capital. Under the **standardised approach,** the Committee desires neither to produce a net increase nor a net decrease, on an average, in minimum regulatory capital, even after accounting for operational risk. Under the **IRB approach**, the Committee's ultimate goals are to ensure that the overall level of regulatory capital is sufficient to address the underlying credit risks and also provides capital incentives relative to the standardised approach, i.e., a reduction in the risk weighted assets of 2% to 3% (foundation IRB approach) and 90% of the capital requirement under foundation approach for advanced IRB approach to encourage banks to adopt IRB approach for providing capital.

10.3 The minimum capital adequacy ratio would continue to be 8% of the risk-weighted assets, which cover capital requirements for market (trading book), credit and operational risks. For **credit risk**, the range of options to estimate capital extends to include a **standardised**, a foundation **IRB** and **advanced IRB** approaches.

Orientation of the IRB Approach

Banks' internal measures of credit risk are based on assessments of the risk characteristics of both the borrower and the specific type of transaction. The probability of default (PD) of a borrower or group of borrowers is the central measurable concept on which the IRB approach is built. The PD of a borrower does not, however, provide the complete picture of the potential credit loss. Banks should also seek to measure how much they will lose should a borrower default on an obligation. This is contingent upon two elements. First, the magnitude of likely loss on the exposure: this is termed the Loss Given Default (LGD), and is expressed as a percentage of the exposure. Secondly, the loss is contingent upon the amount to which the bank was exposed to the borrower at the time of default, commonly expressed as Exposure at Default (EAD). These three components (PD, LGD, EAD) combine to provide a measure of expected intrinsic, or economic, loss. The IRB approach also takes into account the maturity (M) of exposures. Thus, the derivation of risk weights is dependent on estimates of the PD, LGD and, in some cases, M, that are attached to an exposure. These components (PD, LGD, EAD, M) form the basic inputs to the IRB approach, and consequently the capital requirements derived from it.

10.4.1 Standardised Approach

Under the standardised approach, preferential risk weights in the range of 0%, 20%, 50%, 100% and 150% would be assigned on the basis of ratings given by external credit assessment institutions.

10.4.2 IRB Approach

The Committee proposes two approaches—foundation and advanced—as an alternative to standardised approach for assigning preferential risk weights.

Under the ***foundation approach***, banks, which comply with certain minimum requirements viz. comprehensive credit rating system with capability to quantify Probability of Default (PD) could assign preferential risk weights, with the data on Loss Given Default (LGD) and Exposure at Default (EAD) provided by the national supervisors. In order to qualify for adopting the foundation approach, the internal credit rating system should have the following parameters/conditions:

- Each borrower within a portfolio must be assigned the rating before a loan is originated.
- Minimum of 6 to 9 borrower grades for performing loans and a minimum of 2 grades for non-performing loans.
- Meaningful distribution of exposure across grades and not more than 30% of the gross exposures in any one borrower grade.

- Each individual rating assignment must be subject to an independent review or approval by the Loan Review Department.

- Rating must be updated at least on annual basis.

- The Board of Directors must approve all material aspects of the rating and PD estimation.

- Internal and External audit must review annually, the banks' rating system including the quantification of internal ratings.

- Banks should have individual credit risk control units that are responsible for the design, implementation and performance of internal rating systems. These units should be functionally independent.

- Members of staff responsible for rating process should be adequately qualified and trained.

- Internal rating must be explicitly linked with the banks' internal assessment of capital adequacy in line with requirements of Pillar 2.

- Banks must have in place sound stress testing process for the assessment of capital adequacy.

- Banks must have a credible track record in the use of internal ratings at least for **the last 3 years.**

- Banks must have robust systems in place to evaluate the accuracy and consistency with regard to the system, processing and the estimation of PDs.

- Banks must disclose in greater detail the rating process, risk factors, validation etc. of the rating system.

Under the ***advanced approach***, banks would be allowed to use their own estimates of PD, LGD and EAD, which could be validated by the supervisors. Under both the approaches, risk weights would be expressed as a single continuous function of the PD, LGD and EAD. The IRB approach, therefore, does not rely on supervisory determined risk buckets as in the case of standardised approach. The Committee has proposed an IRB approach for retail loan portfolio, having homogenous characteristics distinct from that for the corporate portfolio. The Committee is also working towards developing an appropriate IRB approach relating to project finance.

10.5 The adoption of the New Accord, in the proposed format, requires substantial upgradation of the existing credit risk management systems. The New Accord also provided in-built capital incentives for banks, which are equipped to adopt foundation or advanced IRB approach. Banks may, therefore, upgrade the credit risk management systems for optimising capital.

REFERENCES

Michael Crouhy, Dan Galai and Robert Mark—*Risk Management*, McGraw-Hill Publications 2001.

Anthony Saunders, Marva Millan Cornett—*Financial Institutions and Market*, McGraw-Hill Publications, 4th Edition.

Roger M. Stein: Article on *Benchmarking Default*; Prediction Models: 'Pitfalls and Remedies in Model Validation', New York June 2002.

Deutsche Bank—'*Managing Credit: Global Best Practice*'. Presented at the Credit and Treasury Conference 2002 at Bangalore.

Course Material of 'Risk-Based Supervision for Officers of Commercial Banks'—RBI, August 2002.

Reserve Bank of India 'Guidance Note on Credit Risk Market', 12 October 2002.

Reserve Bank of India 'Guidelines on Country Risk Management', 19 February 2003.

Risk Metrics Group *Risk Management: A Practical Guide*.

Bank for International Settlements '*The New Basel Capital Accord*' January 2001.

Bank for International Settlements '*Consultative Document*', April 2003.

A/04